INTERNET THEORY, TECHNOLOGY AND APPLICATIONS

THE INTERNET OF THINGS (IOT)

APPLICATIONS, TECHNOLOGY, AND PRIVACY ISSUES

INTERNET THEORY, TECHNOLOGY AND APPLICATIONS

Additional books in this series can be found on Nova's website under the Series tab.

Additional e-books in this series can be found on Nova's website under the e-book tab.

INTERNET THEORY, TECHNOLOGY AND APPLICATIONS

THE INTERNET OF THINGS (IOT)

APPLICATIONS, TECHNOLOGY, AND PRIVACY ISSUES

SILVIA WATTS
EDITOR

nova publishers

New York

NOTICE TO THE READER

Library of Congress Cataloging-in-Publication Data

Names: Watts, Silvia, editor.
Title: The Internet of Things (IoT) : applications, technology, and privacy
  issues / editor, Silvia Watts.
Description: Hauppauge, New Yor, : Nova Science Publisher's, Inc., 2016. |
  Series: Internet theory, technology and applications | Includes
  bibliographical references and index.
Identifiers: LCCN 2016000072 (print) | LCCN 2016000673 (ebook) | ISBN
  9781634846264 (hardcover) | ISBN 9781634846448 ()
Subjects: LCSH: Internet of things.
Classification: LCC QA76.5915 .I685 2016 (print) | LCC QA76.5915 (ebook) |
  DDC 004.67/8--dc23
LC record available at http://lccn.loc.gov/2016000072

Published by Nova Science Publishers, Inc. † New York

CONTENTS

PREFACE

Internet of things (IOT) encompasses a wide range of objects and technologies such as radio frequency identification (RFID), near field communication (NFC) and wireless sensor and actuators networks (WSANs). Moreover, IoT encompasses different communication standards, protocols, and data formats so that the IoT environment is heterogeneous, decentralized and complex. The definition of standards and architectures in different levels of abstraction is an essential need of the IoT environments. Chapter One of this book examines architectures, technologies and applications in the Internet of Things. Chapter Two presents the development and implementation of an industrial communication system for remote monitoring and management of industrial processes.

The proliferation of devices with the ability to communicate and transmit information to each other is the basis of the dynamics of IoT, enabling new communication capabilities, data processing and access to information. Perceived as a means to generate both social and economic impacts among the information society, IoT defy the current Internet Governance framework and the role of the public sector. Accordingly, Chapter Three aims to present the current IoT governance scenario, its main challenges, the role of the governments and the need to develop public-private partnerships for technical cooperation in the governance of IoT resources.

In: The Internet of Things (IoT) ISBN: 978-1-63484-626-4
Editor: Silvia Watts © 2016 Nova Science Publishers, Inc.

Chapter 1

INTERNET OF THINGS: ARCHITECTURES, TECHNOLOGIES AND APPLICATIONS

Atslands Rego da Rocha[*], **Flávio R. C. Sousa**[†],
Andrei Bosco B. Torres[‡] **and José Neuman de Souza**[§]
Federal University of Ceará, Campus do Pici, Fortaleza, Brazil

Abstract

The current Internet architecture was designed for sharing resources; therefore, it is not appropriate for Internet of Things (IoT) since it is based on sharing data. The principal purpose of this chapter is to capture the state-of-the-art in Internet of Things architectures, technologies, and applications. A comprehensive review of the existing architectures and applications for IoT is provided here to achieve a better understanding of the open issues in this field. Classification is also performed on the current IoT architectures, and some technologies and services are discussed. Moreover, our vision on the challenges research scope and potential future directions is presented.

Keywords: internet of things, architectures, technologies, applications

AMS Subject Classification: 53D, 37C, 65P

[*]E-mail address: atslands@ufc.br.
[†]E-mail address: sousa@ufc.br.
[‡]E-mail address: andreibosco@virtual.ufc.br.
[§]E-mail address: neuman@ieee.org.

1. Introduction

The current Internet architecture was designed for sharing resources; therefore, it is not appropriate for Internet of Things (IoT) since it is based on sharing data. The key purpose of this chapter is to capture the state-of-the-art in Internet of Things architectures, technologies, and applications. The structure of this chapter is as follows. Section 2, "Reference Architectures", introduces the principles of the IoT reference architectures. Reference architectures denote an abstract and standard concepts able to define an essential set of building blocks for IoT concrete architectures that facilitate the interoperability between heterogeneous IoT systems. Section 3, "Interaction Protocols", presents and compares existing IoT protocols utilized to connect the things such as MQTT (Message Queuing Telemetry Transport), CoAP (Constrained Application Protocol), XMPP (Extensible Messaging and Presence Protocol) and WAMP (Web Application Messaging Protocol). Section 4, "Cloud computing for IoT", discusses general considerations about how cloud computing architecture meets the challenges of flexibility, extensibility and economic viability of IoT. On demand provision of the cloud resources used to power IoT architecture is an important issue on the scalability of the architecture. Section 5 describes the fog computing that extends the cloud computing paradigm to the edge of the network enabling a new set of applications and services. Fog computing meets the requirements of IoT such as mobility support, geo-distribution, location awareness and low latency. Section 6, "Autonomic Management", presents the autonomic management as a natural technology to enable self-management in IoT devices to minimize the degree of the human intervention required. Self-* properties (self-organization, self-configuration, self-optimizing, self-healing) are necessary for a massive number of devices. However, IoT devices have some restrictions e.g., energy, processing, memory, among others. Section 7, "IoT Applications", presents some current key IoT applications fields. Section 8, "Challenges", presents some current gaps and IoT challenges that need to be solved. An example is data collected from IoT environment be huge because of everything will be connected to the Internet. Moreover, finally, Section 9 presents the conclusion of the chapter.

2.   Reference Architectures

Internet of things encompasses a wide range of objects and technologies such as radio frequency identification (RFID), near field communication (NFC) and wireless sensor and actuators networks (WSANs). Moreover, IoT encompasses different communication standards, protocols, and data formats so that the IoT environment is heterogeneous, decentralized and complex. Therefore, the definition of standards and architectures at various levels of abstraction is an essential need of the IoT environments.

A reference model denotes an abstract framework that comprises a minimal set of unifying concepts, axioms, and relationships for understanding significant relationships between the entities of an environment [1]. A reference model enables the development of reference architectures with different levels of abstraction and independent of specific technologies, implementations, or other concrete details.

An IoT reference architecture can be defined as an abstract and standard concept able to define a set of essential building blocks for IoT concrete architectures to facilitate the interoperability between heterogeneous IoT systems. A single reference architecture design cannot be used to construct all IoT applications, but heterogeneous IoT reference architectures have to coexist to be suitable for the diverse and possible concrete implementations.

Standardization efforts have recently been made. China Communications Standards Association (CCSA) proposed an IoT reference model [2] and an open and general architecture. The CCSA reference model consists of four layers (sensing, network, business, and application) to meet the specific needs of the applications.

Another architectural reference model is proposed by the members of the IoT-A (Internet of Things Architecture) project [1]. The IoT ARM [1] constitutes a foundation for the creation of open and interoperable systems and integrated environments and platforms. It consists of a reference architecture and an essential set of features to construct IoT concrete architectures. Such reference architecture provides a joint use of architectural views and perspectives in architecture descriptions for designing and implementing a concrete architecture.

An architectural view can be defined as a representation of structural aspects of architecture, composed of a collection of patterns, templates, and conventions. Relevant examples of views proposed by the reference architecture of the

---

[1] http://www.iot-a.eu/.

IoT ARM are functional, information and deployment and operation views. The functional view provides a description of the functional components, however, does not describe the interactions among them. This fact is due to the number of arrangements of the functional components, and also their invocation is practically infinite [1]. The information view provides both static information structure and dynamic information flow. The information view describes the components that handle the information, the flow of such information through the system and its life cycle into the system. The deployment and operation view addresses how an IoT system can be realized by selecting suitable technologies and making them communicate and operate. Besides, the deployment and operation view provides guidelines to drive developers through the design alternatives of the actual implementation of the system.

An architectural perspective can be defined as a set of activities, tactics, and guidelines for ensuring that a system exhibits one or more quality properties (e.g., performance, security, scalability) that require consideration across some architectural views. IoT ARM provides perspectives regarded as the most important non-functional requirements for IoT systems: evolution and interoperability; availability and resilience; reliability, security, and privacy; and performance and scalability.

3. Interaction Protocols

Apart from IoT architectures, a great effort from the research and stakeholder community is related to the protocol suites. Some of the known standard protocols utilized to interconnect the things and end-user applications to the Internet of Things are MQTT (Message Queuing Telemetry Transport), CoAP (Constrained Application Protocol), XMPP (Extensible Messaging and Presence Protocol) and WAMP (Web Application Messaging Protocol). Table 1 resumes the key features of the IoT message protocols.

3.1. MQTT

Initially created by IBM in 1999, MQ Telemetry Transport (MQTT) was formerly known as WebSphere MQTT, or MQ Integrator SCADA Device Protocol. MQTT is an open messaging protocol designed for machine-to-machine (M2M) communication, to cope with high latency, unstable communication, and low bandwidth. Such protocol is being highly adopted by numerous companies

Table 1. IoT Message Protocols

	MQTT	MQTT-SN	CoAP	WAMP	XMPP
Latest version	3.1.1	1.2	RFC 7252	Draft 02	RFC 6120 to 6122 (Core)
Specification body	OASIS	-	IETF	IETF (Draft)	IETF
Transport layer	TCP, Websocket	UDP	UDP	Websocket	TCP, HTTP[1], Websocket[1]
Messaging pattern	Pubsub	Pubsub	Request-response[2]	Pubsub, RPC	Request-response, Pubsub[1] RPC[1]
Message encoding format	Agnostic	Binary	Binary	JSON, MsgPack, raw TCP	XML
Security	Username + password auth	-	DTLS	TLS	TLS, SASL

[1] Available through extensions

[2] There is a draft specification that adds support for pubsub

focused on IoT, and, according to [3], Director of Marketing for the Eclipse Foundation, "It seems to me that MQTT has now become a defacto 'must be supported standard' for any serious IoT solution provider". The MQTT protocol was standardized by OASIS in 2013 and currently is on version 3.1.1 [4], being royalty free since 2010.

MQTT uses TCP as its communication protocol, and the publisher/subscriber paradigm as it messaging pattern. It is similar to the logic of an RSS feed: a client subscribes to a topic and receives data as it is pushed by the publisher. The main difference is that everything is controlled by a hub called *broker*. The broker manages all the data and communication, decoupling the producer from the client, where only the broker address have to be known, and permitting 'one-to-one', 'one-to-many' and 'many-to-many' communication.

On the security side, as of version 3.1.1, MQTT doesn't implement any kind of encryption, relying on username and password authentication only, although SSL can be used independently.

MQTT main features are:

- Publisher/subscriber pattern;

- Three levels of Quality of Service (QoS):

    - QoS 0 *at most once*: best effort, no delivery guarantee;

- QoS 1 *at least once*: delivery guarantee, but possible duplication;
- QoS 2 *exactly once*: delivery guarantee with no duplication.

- Retained messages: messages can be retained on the broker and relayed to new subscribers when they connect;

- Last Will and Testament (LWT): clients can provide the broker a message to be relayed in case of an unexpected disconnection;

- Data agnostic: the MQTT standard doesn't enforce any data format.

3.2. MQTT-SN

MQTT-SN (MQTT for Sensor Networks, formerly known as MQTT-S) is an extension of the MQTT protocol focused on embedded devices that communicate on non-TCP networks, adopting UDP as its network protocol. It implements most of MQTT features, with a few exceptions, most notably:

- Quality of service (QoS) level -1, where no connection is attempted and the message is sent blindly;

- Topic name is replaced by topic id, to reduce message length and save bandwidth;

- New offline keep-alive procedure to save battery life.

The MQTT-SN architecture is made of three components: MQTT-SN clients, MQTT-SN gateways and MQTT-SN forwarders. Gateways receive data from clients using the MQTT-SN protocol and pass them to MQTT brokers using the regular MQTT protocol while forwarders allow data to be relayed to a gateway located on a different network. A MQTT-SN gateway might be integrated with a regular MQTT server, and be set to aggregate data from various publishers or to relay them as is.

Unfortunately, MQTT-SN still hasn't gained wide adoption by the community or private companies[2], with RSMB[3] (Really Small Message Broker), a bro-

---

[2]HiveMQ position about MQTT-SN: `https://groups.google.com/forum/#!topic/hivemq/xcuqYjUnzR4`.

[3]IBM developerWorks - Really Small Message Broker: `https://www.ibm.com/developerworks/community/groups/service/html/communityview?communityUuid=d5bedadd-e46f-4c97-af89-22d65ffee070`.

ker originally created by IBM and that served as basis for the Mosquitto broker, being the only one that supports it.

3.3. CoAP

CoAP (Constrained Application Protocol) was created based on the HTTP RESTful architecture to allow highly constrained devices to be accessible through URLs and allow clients to use methods like GET, PUT, POST, and DELETE. CoAP was standardized on 2014 by IETF as RFC 7252, and it was designed to be extensible, with some other RFCs implementing additional functionalities[4].

CoAP messages can be set as 'non-confirmable' (NON) or 'confirmable' (CON), similar to MQTT QoS 0 and QoS 1, respectively. NON messages don't require any confirmation of delivery while CON messages must be confirmed by the receiver. Since UDP doesn't have a message delivery confirmation method, CoAP implements its own method for confirmation and retransmission.

Unlike MQTT, CoAP follows a standard client/server model where the client connects directly to the server producing the data. To secure connections, CoAP supports Datagram Transport Layer Security (DTLS), a stream-oriented protocol based on TLS.

It's main features are:

- Low overhead;

- REST model;

- Optional UDP reliability;

- Support for DTLS;

- URI and Content-type support;

- HTTP mapping.

---

[4]e.g., RFC 7390: group communication; RFC: 7641: Observing Resources in the Constrained Application Protocol.

3.4.   XMPP

Originally called Jabber, the Extensible Messaging and Presence Protocol (XMPP) was created in 1998 aimed to be an open technology for instant messaging services, using XML streaming at its core. In 2004, a group of specifications were formally published by IETF as the core of XMPP, and as of 2015 they were super-seeded by the following RFCs: 6120, 6121 and 6122.

In 2001, the XMPP Standards Foundation (XSF) was founded to be an independent non-profit entity to support the development of XMPP extensions (XEP). Several of them have gained large adoption by the community, such as multi-user chat (MUC), voice and video calls and file transfer.

XMPP main features are:

- decentralized architecture: there is no centralized authoritative server, anyone can run an XMPP server;

- flexibility: numerous extensions, currently over 170 XEPs (including the draft, experimental and proposed specifications).

Regarding IoT, the XMPP community started a wiki document[5] listing relevant XEPs, examples, implementations, but it is still at an early stage.

3.5.   WAMP

The Web Application Messaging Protocol (WAMP) is the latest addition to the lineup, created in 2012 and currently published as a draft as an IETF standard [5]. WAMPs goal is to be a "Unified Application Routing", uniting the publisher/subscriber (PubSub) model with remote procedure calls (RPC), over the WebSocket protocol.

WAMP uses the publish/subscribe structure (Publisher - Broker - Subscriber) and applies it to RPC, where the Caller calls are routed to the Callee by a Dealer. So, a WAMP router combines the functionalities of a Broker and a RPC Dealer, allowing applications to receive data from a sensor and control an actuator through a single protocol.

---

[5]XMPP Tech Pages - IoT Systems: http://wiki.xmpp.org/web/Tech_pages/ IoT_systems.

4. Cloud Computing for IoT

Economic factors are causing significant growth in infrastructure for providing computing as a service. This concept is known as Cloud Computing, in which companies and individuals are able to rent processing and storage capacity, instead of making big investments to construct and provision a large scale computing platform. These services are typically hosted in data centers, using shared hardware for processing and storage.

Scalability, elasticity, pay-per-use pricing, and economies of scale are the major reasons for the successful and widespread adoption of cloud infrastructures. One major benefit claimed for cloud computing is elasticity, that adjusts the system's capacity at runtime by adding and removing resources without service interruption in order to handle the workload variation [6]. These resources can be acquired quickly, in some cases even automatically, to meet the increases and decreases of the workloads. For cloud users, the resources available appear to be unlimited and can be purchased in any amount and at any time.

Infrastructure as a service (IaaS), Platform as a service (PaaS), and Software as a service (SaaS) are the classical categories of cloud services, although there are other proposed categories such as Database as a Service (DBaaS), Cache as a Service (CaaS), Unified Communications as a Service (UCaaS). In fact, cloud services are becoming so popular that some authors mention the category Everything as a Service (XaaS) [7].

On the other hand, the Internet of Things (IoT) represents a worldwide network of heterogeneous cyber-physical objects such as sensors, actuators, smart devices, smart objects, RFID, embedded computers. These objects, which have identities, physical attributes, and a communication interface for service provision, are uniquely addressable and based on standard communication protocols [8].

In general, the devices on the Internet of Things have resource constraints and, therefore, are traditionally designed to support specific applications. The strong coupling between the network and the application limits the use of resources and data collected by the devices.

IoT is characterized by a very high heterogeneity of devices, technologies, and protocols. Therefore, scalability, interoperability, reliability, efficiency, availability, and security can be very difficult to obtain. The integration with the Cloud solves most of these problems, also providing additional features such as ease-of-access, ease-of-use, and reduced deployment costs [9] .

Cloud computing makes it possible for the IoT devices even with limited computational capabilities, perform intricate computations required for effective performance of the assigned task [10]. Cloud computing promises high reliability, scalability and autonomy to provide ubiquitous access, dynamic resource discovery and composability required for the next generation Internet of Things applications. Consumers will be able to choose the service level by changing the Quality of Service parameters [11].

The things need only to have the sensors and the actuators, and their decision-making capabilities can be facilitated by the almost infinite computational capabilities of the cloud. Thus, cloud computing can be customized to support a distributed real-time system for the management and analysis of IoT things and data streams generated by IoT things.

For example, sensing service providers can join the network and offer their data using a storage cloud; analytic tool developers can provide their software tools; artificial intelligence experts can provide their data mining and machine learning tools useful in converting information to knowledge and finally computer graphics designer can offer a variety of visualization tools [12]. Thus, it is important to develop solutions for integrating ubiquitous sensing devices, and the cloud provides great flexibility and scalability for IoT systems. Sensing devices can join the network and provide data to the cloud, and the cloud can analyze the data.

In the context of IoT, the sensors collect a large volume of data and need to store and process them. However, these sensors have limited resources. Thus, the cloud can receive the sensor data for storage, processing and analysis. Due to the large volume of devices and data, it is important to cloud platforms using scalable data management solutions (e.g., NoSQL systems), allowing data analysis and generating higher added value. In many situations, the analytical process must be efficient, real-time, requiring a greater amount of cloud resources that can be achieved by elasticity.

In many scenarios, it is important to reduce the power consumption of the devices. To address this problem one may use offloading techniques using the cloud. For example, wireless sensor network typically consists of low cost, low power, and energy-constrained sensors. Each operation, calculation and intercommunication consume the node energy.

Thus, one can keep the local resources of mobile devices, especially energy resources, which are the most scarce. Furthermore, mobility is an essential point in the integration of IoT with the cloud; it should be provided transparent access to cloud environments.

In addition to providing the entire virtual infrastructure for computing and storage applications, it allows you to analyze data collected from the things and assist in the decision-making process.

A potential limitation of clouds for IOTs is that the user has less influence on the Thingánd to ensure reliable services, it is thus necessary to choose cloud service providers carefully and to contract the quality of service demanded both by the user as well as the manufacturer of the Thing. Besides, deploying IOT on clouds might cause problems of connectivity.

Depending on factors such as their position or a current environment, local computing resources such as sensors, human-computer interfaces, and other systems embedded into objects might periodically either have network access without sufficient bandwidth or even none at all. Moreover authorized access to IoT cloud sensor data and services without relaxing user privacy is also a challenging task [10].

5.   Fog Computing

Fog Computing is a paradigm that extends Cloud computing and services to the edge of the network [13]. Fog can be differentiated from Cloud by its proximity to end-users. According to Vaquero and Rodero-Merino [14], *fog computing is a scenario where a huge number of heterogeneous (wireless and sometimes autonomous) ubiquitous and decentralized devices communicate and potentially cooperate among them and with the network to perform storage and processing tasks without the intervention of third-parties.*

The emerging trends in networking such as large distributed Internet-connected sensor networks IoT) mobile data networks, and also real-time streaming applications have characteristics that cannot be satisfied by cloud computing [13]. Fog provides compute, storage and network similar to Cloud. In contrast to the cloud, Fog presents specific characteristics: edge location and location awareness implying low latency; geographical distribution and a vast number of nodes in contrast to centralized Cloud; support for mobility through wireless access and improves the quality of service (QoS) and real-time applications.

Thus, fog computing is the most suitable communication model compared to cloud computing where information processing takes place deep within the Internet [15] and address the mobility problem when the things move fast. These characteristics improvement the development of many scenarios, such as smart grid, vehicular networks, wireless sensor networks, IoT, and software-defined networks (SDNs) that require faster processing with less delay and real-time interactions.

For scenarios requiring high reliability and/or predictable latency, the goal should be to locate the intelligence where it is needed in the network, or even be embedded on them, thereby enabling higher reliability and localized closed-loop control [16]. It improves the processing and storage of data for analysis and making real-time decisions essential for many applications.

To increase the use of Fog computing, it is necessary to address some challenges, such as programmability, accountability, standardization, management, discovery/sync, compute/storage limit and security [14].

6. Autonomic Management

The purpose of autonomic management is to handle heterogeneity and complexity of the systems. The fundamental principle of autonomic management is to enable self-* properties (self-organization, self-configuration, self-optimizing, self-healing) in the devices aiming self-management and a low degree of direct human intervention. Thus, autonomic systems can obtain a certain level of flexibility and adapt themselves to new contexts, user needs or environmental changes.

The standard definition for an autonomic system based on IBM's autonomic framework [17] includes two entities: managed resource and autonomic manager. The managed resource is the end system and comprises sensors and effectors. Sensors are responsible for collecting data from a managed resource, as well as the environment while effectors are responsible for sending commands to the managed device. Thus, managers can monitor the environment through the sensors and execute that action through effectors. The knowledge base consists of policies, action plans, among other items.

The autonomic manager provides a control loop called MAPE-K: monitoring, analysis, processing, execution and knowledge base. The monitor function is responsible for collecting data from sensors. The analyze function allows the autonomic manager to analyze the data, comparing this with historical and current data, rules and beliefs, and perform diagnosis. The plan function provides a guide to necessary actions with the help of policies, to achieve goals and objectives. Finally, the execute function controls the execution of the pre-defined plans through effectors.

A self-managed internet of things is a challenge due to the specific characteristics of IoT such as high dynamicity, real-time nature and resources constraints (energy, processing, memory). However, exists many efforts on how to adapt and tailor existing research on autonomic management area to the specific characteristics of the internet of the things. An example is the ISOS [18], an effort to tailor a self-organization scheme to smart objects in IoT environments to build scalable and dynamic systems.

ISOS [18] is an intelligent self-organizing system for the IoT inspired by the endocrine regulating mechanism of blood glucose regulation in the human body. Each node in the network establishes an autonomous area, where such node can effectively cooperate with its peers and to adapt and to self-control according to its status and changing circumstances.

Smart objects in IoT environments have some essential requirements [19]: (i) be identifiable, (ii) to communicate and (iii) to interact among themselves, with end-users or other entities in the network. Besides, the services also need to be adaptable to diverse contexts providing an additional degree of flexibility. Taking these inherent characteristics and expected functionality of the IoT into account, a self-organization scheme should satisfy the four requirements described below [18]:

- Decentralized infrastructure based on autonomy. The basic idea is each node in the IoT to be implemented with a certain degree of autonomy. Thus, such nodes can collect information about respective environments and make decisions for their behaviors. The data also can be exchanged among nodes in a fully or partially (restricted to a limited area) decentralized form.

- Efficient collaboration based on ubiquitous data exchanging and sharing. The member nodes in the IoT environment should be able to collect information from their neighbors. Intelligent services including the participation of multiple nodes with different categories, functions and contents can also be offered.

- Energy-optimized solution based on working status switchover. The minimization of the energy spent for communication/computing purposes is always a primary concern for the IoT entities [18] [19]. A well-designed strategy should not only decrease the energy consumption of the nodes but also satisfy the nodes requirements to conduct their functionalities in a satisfactory way.

- Intelligent service discovery based on adaptive response to the demands. Each node in an IoT environment has to organize autonomously and provide basic means for sharing data and performing the coordinated tasks.

7. IoT Applications

The IoT technology encompasses smart and connected objects. The possibility to communicate an object with others and to collect the information about the environment (e.g., natural phenomena, medical parameters, or user habits) enables a broad range of application markets. Many authors categorize the IoT applications into different domains or fields [19] [20] [11]. However, there is almost a consensus about the following key applications domains: industrial, smart city, and health/well-being domain. These domains partially overlap themselves since some applications can be shared between them. For example, applications to tracking goods are common between the industrial and the health well-being domains since they can track foods or pharmaceutical products [20].

7.1. Industrial Domain

The industrial domain encompasses industrial activities involving commercial or financial transactions between entities. Relevant examples are logistic and management of the product lifetime and agriculture and breeding.

- Logistic and management of the product lifetime. Radio frequency identification technologies provide the identification and support for tracking goods in real time, including the entire objectś life cycle. These abilities support applications such as inventory and stock control in stores and markets. Furthermore, sensors can monitor the production processes and final product quality. For example, RFID devices can be used to identify and track the product, while the bio-sensors can monitor parameters such as temperature and bacterial composition to guarantee required quality of the final product [19].

- Agriculture and breeding. Specific applications developed to monitor the processes of the agricultural production. For example, IoT technology can provide precision irrigation and fertigation to improve the rational use of the water and a suitable injection of fertilizers into an irrigation system, respectively. IoT systems also allow to identify and trace animals aiming to obtain valuable information about the animal status such as localization, age, diseases, vaccines performed, temperature, weight, among others. By using IoT, such applications can ensure the quality of both the plant and animal origin products intended for human consumption.

7.2. Smart City Domain

Smart Cities are cyber-physical eco-systems emerging by deploying advanced communication infrastructure and novel services over city-wide scenarios [19]. The main objectives of the smart city domain are optimizing the sustainability of the physical city infrastructures, such as road networks and power grids, and improving the quality of life for the citizens. Diverse applications can be applied in smart cities scenarios such as smart homes (buildings) and environmental monitoring.

- Smart Homes or Buildings: Sensors and actuators can be employed for monitoring of the resources consumption and actuating on the controlled resources according to users need such as switching on/off lighting and heating tasks. A great advantage of this kind of application is reducing the resources consumption associated with the buildings such as electricity and water. Beside of the impact in economic terms, another advantage can also be societal impact since smart buildings field can reduce the carbon footprint associated with buildings, which are key contributors to the global greenhouse gas emissions [19].

- Environmental monitoring: applications have the ability to sense natural phenomena and processes such as temperature, the wind, rainfall, and river height. Some examples are fire detection, natural disaster detection (tsunamis and earthquakes). Environmental monitoring: applications have the ability to sense natural phenomena and processes such as temperature, the wind, rainfall, and river height. Typical examples of environmental monitoring applications are fire detection, natural disaster detection (tsunamis and earthquakes). This kind of application can handle and process a large amount of heterogeneous data collected from sensors in real-time. Thus, in the case of disasters, environmental monitoring applications can provide a rapid response mitigating the damage to the buildings, nature or people.

7.3.   Health Well-Being Domain

Health well-being domain enables common people to get involved in the government decisions aiming to improve health and social care areas. Relevant examples of applications fields are health care, assisted living, and well-being solutions.

- Medical and Healthcare: Wireless Body Area Networks (WBANs) are currently used to monitor vital functions of the patients (e.g., temperature, blood pressure) to transmit a medical report to remote centers. The processing of the data originated from these various sensors could provide a holistic vision of the patient health and prevent the onset of health problems [19].

- Assisted living. Wearable sensors (e.g., accelerometers, gyroscopes) can monitor patient activities in their living environments tracking their lifestyles such as regular exercises and habits. Moreover, this kind of applications allows the condition monitoring of elderly or disabled population to support independent living.

7.4.   IoT-Aided Robotics Applications

The ongoing advance in Internet of Things and the growing diffusion of robots in many daily activities makes IoT-aided robotics applications a tangible reality of our upcoming future [21]. IoT-aided robotics (possible) applications can be also classified in domains mentioned above:

- Industrial domain: applications involves the use of robots to support activities such as surveillance, autonomous management of equipment and instruments, and the immediate reaction to the danger situations such as harmful chemicals in the river, among others.

- Smart City domain: applications involves support for secured and automatized building environments; access control in restricted areas; access preclusion to unauthorized persons; assistance during panic events.

- Health well-being domain: robots can be used for rehabilitation and automatic assistance of monitored patients with impaired motor or cognitive skills. In this kind of application, robots enhance existing therapeutic systems improving the functional recovery and assessment of patients [21]. In assisted living applications, the use of robots can promote independent living of disabled and elderly people (e.g., people movement monitoring).

8.   IoT Challenges

Internet of Things promises the interconnection of a myriad of smart things that will be deployed worldwide to provide services to people and things. However, the traditional Internet architecture based on sharing resources design is not appropriate for Internet of things based on sharing data. Some open challenges [22] [2] [11] are listed below:

1. One of the most important challenges is security (privacy, integrity, availability and encryption). Things can be deployed at large scale in IoT environments, and existing security architecture is designed from the perspective of people communication, not being suitable to IoT system. Data integrity, privacy, data ownership, energy-efficient cryptography algorithms, legal and liability issues have to be addressed accordingly.

2. The development and deployment of self-aware things, autonomic things with self-* properties enabled, is a challenge due to the specific characteristics of IoT environments.

3. Technological and semantic interoperability is significantly more challenging for the IoT environments than traditional internet environment due to (i) they have different technological capabilities, and (ii) they can connect people with things and things with things. This seamless interaction between people with heterogeneous devices generates a large amount of shared heterogeneous information. Thus, improvements have to be made regarding the information model to the devices interpret the shared information correctly and act accordingly. Moreover, for full interoperability, standards for IoT must be created and broadly used. IoT reference architectures should be defined, and then, IoT concrete architectures must be specified based on such IoT reference architectures. This

standardization can facilitate the interoperability between heterogeneous IoT systems.

4. By default, IoT is multi-service, providing different applications or services. Thus, multiple traffic types (e.g., throughput and delay tolerant elastic traffic classes) will be transmitted within the network, and many applications/services will need quality of service (QoS) compromise. Moreover, IoT involves shared wireless media, data, and tools available on clouds, which is already an environment needs QoS requirements. Therefore, providing quality of service in IoT environments can be a hard challenge.

5. A large amount of data will be transmitted from (billion or trillion) heterogeneous things to the IoT. Exploring the large volumes of data and extracting useful information from a complex sensing environment at different spatial and temporal resolutions in a fast and effective way is a challenging research problem [11] [22]. The key characteristics of resource constraints in sensor networks (and RFID systems) and high capacity for applications in cloud computing create novel challenges for proposals of adaptive and distributed solutions.

6. In general, heterogeneous sensing devices taking part in the IoT demands the use of multiple sensing modalities and are not connected to an unlimited power supply. Therefore, efficient energy sensing is a conditioning factor in the design and operation of IoT environments. Therefore, many IoT solutions based on WSN or RFID have to be oriented to low-energy consumption. While such technologies do not still provide enough resources, this is a broad research challenge. Approaches proposed for WSNs [23] and other low-power technologies can be adapted to deal with the requirements of the IoT.

Conclusion

The internet of things paradigm encompasses several technologies aiming at connecting anything, to be accessed at any time from anywhere. This chapter reviews the state of the art in IoT paradigm, describing standards and architecture models, analyzing different interaction protocols and implementations, to finally come up with a general description of technologies and applications.

Moreover, a review of the challenges and open research issues that must be solved to make real the IoT.

References

[1] Alessandro Bassi, Martin Bauer, Martin Fiedler, Thorsten Kramp, Rob van Kranenburg, Sebastian Lange, and Stefan Meissner. Enabling things to talk, 2013.

[2] Shanzhi Chen, Hui Xu, Dake Liu, Bo Hu, and Hucheng Wang. A vision of iot: Applications, challenges, and opportunities with china perspective. *Internet of Things Journal, IEEE*, 1(4):349–359, Aug 2014.

[3] Ian Skerrett. Case Study MQTT: Why Open Source and Open Standards Drive Adoption. https://ianskerrett.wordpress.com/2015/03/04/case-study-mqtt-why-open-source-and-open-standards-drives-adoption/, March 2015. Acessed November 16, 2015.

[4] MQTT Version 3.1.1 OASIS Standard. OASIS Standard, October 2014. http://docs.oasis-open.org/mqtt/mqtt/v3.1.1/os/mqtt-v3.1.1-os.html. Latest version: http://docs.oasis-open.org/mqtt/mqtt/v3.1.1/mqtt-v3.1.1.html.

[5] The Web Application Messaging Protocol. Internet-Draft, October 2015. *IETF Secretariat*, http://www.ietf.org/internet-drafts/draft-oberstet-hybi-tavendo-wamp-02.txt.

[6] EmanuelFerreira Coutinho, FlvioRubens de Carvalho Sousa, PauloAntonioLeal Rego, DanieloGonalves Gomes, and JoseNeuman de Souza. Elasticity in cloud computing: a survey. *annals of telecommunications - annales des tlcommunications*, 70(7-8):289–309, 2015.

[7] Maristella Ribas, C.G. Furtado, Jos Neuman de Souza, Giovanni Cordeiro Barroso, Anto Moura, Alberto S. Lima, and Flvio R.C. Sousa. A petri net-based decision-making framework for assessing cloud services adoption: The use of spot instances for cost reduction. *Journal of Network and Computer Applications*, 57:102 – 118, 2015.

[8] G. Fortino, A. Guerrieri, W. Russo, and C. Savaglio. Integration of agent-based and cloud computing for the smart objects-oriented iot. In *Computer Supported Cooperative Work in Design (CSCWD), Proceedings of the 2014 IEEE 18th International Conference on*, pages 493–498, May 2014.

[9] Alessio Botta, Walter de Donato, Valerio Persico, and Antonio Pescape. Integration of cloud computing and internet of things: A survey. *Future Generation Computer Systems*, pages –, 2015.

[10] P. Parwekar. From internet of things towards cloud of things. In *Computer and Communication Technology (ICCCT), 2011 2nd International Conference on*, pages 329–333, Sept 2011.

[11] Jayavardhana Gubbi, Rajkumar Buyya, Slaven Marusic, and Marimuthu Palaniswami. Internet of things (iot): A vision, architectural elements, and future directions. *Future Generation Computer Systems*, 29(7):1645–1660, 2013.

[12] Jayavardhana Gubbi, Rajkumar Buyya, Slaven Marusic, and Marimuthu Palaniswami. Internet of things (iot): A vision, architectural elements, and future directions. *Future Gener. Comput. Syst.*, 29(7):1645–1660, September 2013.

[13] Flavio Bonomi, Rodolfo Milito, Jiang Zhu, and Sateesh Addepalli. Fog computing and its role in the internet of things. In *Proceedings of the First Edition of the MCC Workshop on Mobile Cloud Computing*, MCC '12, pages 13–16, New York, NY, USA, 2012. ACM.

[14] Luis M. Vaquero and Luis Rodero-Merino. Finding your way in the fog: Towards a comprehensive definition of fog computing. *SIGCOMM Comput. Commun. Rev.*, 44(5):27–32, October 2014.

[15] Kirak Hong, David Lillethun, Umakishore Ramachandran, Beate Ottenwälder, and Boris Koldehofe. Mobile fog: A programming model for large-scale applications on the internet of things. In *Proceedings of the Second ACM SIGCOMM Workshop on Mobile Cloud Computing*, MCC '13, pages 15–20, New York, NY, USA, 2013. ACM.

[16] M. Yannuzzi, R. Milito, R. Serral-Gracia, D. Montero, and M. Nemirovsky. Key ingredients in an iot recipe: Fog computing, cloud computing, and more fog computing. In *Computer Aided Modeling and Design of Communication Links and Networks (CAMAD), 2014 IEEE 19th International Workshop on*, pages 325–329, Dec 2014.

[17] Jeffrey O Kephart and David M Chess. The vision of autonomic computing. *Computer*, 36(1):41–50, 2003.

[18] Yongsheng Ding, Yanling Jin, Lihong Ren, and Kuangrong Hao. An intelligent self-organization scheme for the internet of things. *Computational Intelligence Magazine, IEEE*, 8(3):41–53, Aug 2013.

[19] Daniele Miorandi, Sabrina Sicari, Francesco De Pellegrini, and Imrich Chlamtac. Internet of things: Vision, applications and research challenges. *Ad Hoc Networks*, 10(7):1497–1516, 2012.

[20] Eleonora Borgia. The internet of things vision: Key features, applications and open issues. *Computer Communications*, 54:1–31, 2014.

[21] LA Grieco, A Rizzo, S Colucci, S Sicari, G Piro, D Di Paola, and G Boggia. Iot-aided robotics applications: Technological implications, target domains and open issues. *Computer Communications*, 54:32–47, 2014.

[22] Feng Chen, Pan Deng, Jiafu Wan, Daqiang Zhang, Athanasios V Vasilakos, and Xiaohui Rong. Data mining for the internet of things: literature review and challenges. *International Journal of Distributed Sensor Networks*, 501:431047, 2015.

[23] A. R. Rocha, L. Pirmez, F. C. Delicato, E. Lemos, I. Santos, D. G. Gomes, and J. N. de Souza. Wsns clustering based on semantic neighborhood relationships. *Computer Networks*, 56(5):1627–1645, 2012.

In: The Internet of Things (IoT)   ISBN: 978-1-63484-626-4
Editor: Silvia Watts   © 2016 Nova Science Publishers, Inc.

Chapter 2

INDUSTRIAL WIRELESS SENSORS NETWORK WITH AN IOT-INTERNET OF THINGS-PLATFORM

Juan Felipe Corso[1,], Yeison Julian Camargo[2*] and Leonardo Juan Ramirez[2]*

[1]Mechatronics Engineering, Military Nueva Granada University,
Bogotá Colombia
[2]Telecommunications Engineering, Military Nueva Granada University,
Bogotá Colombia

ABSTRACT

In this work we present the development and implementation of an industrial communication system for remote monitoring and management of industrial processes. The system is implemented based on the IoT (Internet of Things) model. This way, we connected multiple sensors to a wireless system which sends the information to a cloud server. Base on the fact that the gathered data from the sensors is available on the internet, we are able to visualize, analyze and download the data from all over the world. Thus, we additionally developed an SCADA system which obtains the information from the cloud server and it supervises the average values not pass a threshold value. If the value is above the threshold, we communicate the SCADA (Supervisory Control and Data

* Corresponding author: juan.corso@unimilitar.edu.co, yeison.camargo@unimilitar.edu.co

Acquisition) system with a PLC (Programmable Logic Controller) that performs an action. Furthermore, the SCADA system allows to manually control the PLC. Finally, we present the mathematical modeling of the implemented network by using Petri models and we analyze the networking system by using network packet measurements and protocol analyzers.

INTRODUCTION

A principal aspect in the industrial automation processes is the signaling obtained from the multiple sensor that allows to evaluate the state of the process. Currently this is mainly done through sensors connected with wired lines to the control system [1]. However, there are multiple scenarios where the wire is difficult to install, because of the machines (rotating machines) or the places with difficult access (oil fields) [2][3]. Thus, it is necessary to develop, design and implement measurement systems that allows to send the information in real time (taking into account the delays in the communication) through wireless technology with the possibility to monitor it from anywhere in the world [4]-[8] by the internet [9]. IWSNs (Industrial Wireless Sensor Networks) [10]-[12] are increasing their popularity in the industrial automation field. Thus, offering multiple advantages over the traditional wired installations for industrial monitoring and control systems such as easy implementation for: hostile and difficult access environments [5][6] and hard to wire machines, e.g., milling machines, grinding machines [8]. The implemented network needs to be modeled to prove its robustness and predict possible failure points. This can be done through the use of Petri Nets. In fact multiples studies with Petri nets has been implemented for the industrial field but they do not involve wireless sensors [13]-[16][29] connected to the internet.

Additionally the concept of the IoT [17]-[19] (Internet of Things) is taking a huge importance with the implementation of new technologies such as IPv6, which offers a big addressing scheme (allowing address assignation to each sensor in the network, thus a unique identification of the sensor in a network) and inbuilt security mechanism for encryption and authentication of the information (IPsec) [20] [21].

Based on the aspects mentioned above our research project implements an IWSN that allows the transmission of the information from the sensors to the Internet (or cloud) through wireless technology. The implemented network was modeled and simulated with Petri Nets. The system represents a scaled model that can be implemented in an industrial environment. It measures the temperature and gather the information in a central point located in the internet according to the IoT concept which then can be manipulated and control from all over the world, in our case we developed a SCADA (Supervision Control and Data Acquisition) system which controls a PLC according the information obtained from the central platform in the cloud.

The current work is organized as follows: Section I describes the implemented network topology. Section II describes the developed mathematical model under the Petri Nets concept. Section III describes a network analysis performed in the implemented IWSN. Section IV describes the implemented IoT platform for data gathering and worldwide control of the system. Section V describes the development and implementation of the SCADA system for the PLC communication and control. Section VI describes the results obtained in the mathematical model simulation with the Petri Nets and Section VII shows the conclusions and future work.

1. WIRELESS COMMUNICATION SYSTEM AND IoT (INTERNET OF THINGS)

In this section, we will describe the communication system built to gather, process and analyze the data from the sensors which is passing through the internet, the SCADA system and finally performs an action with a PLC. The system receives some input of data from three different sensors, the data is gathered by an Arduino with a wireless shield that sends the information to a main router.

Then, the information is sent over the internet to a central system in the cloud (Xively) [25] that stores and plot the data. Once the information is available in the cloud, we developed a SCADA system that constantly is in communication with the Internet and obtains the information from the central system (Xively) then evaluates the information to decide whether or not perform an action with the PLC, furthermore the SCADA system plots the data and it allows the end user to manually perform an action. We show a general diagram that explains the multiple steps involved in the communication system (refer to Figure 1).

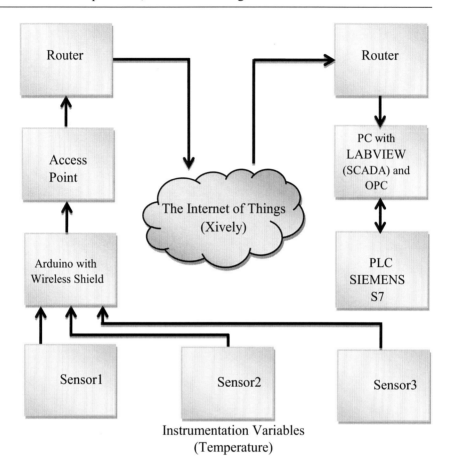

Figure 1. System Block Diagram.

The figure 2, shows the existing communication from the sensors to the PLC which can be located remotely from the sensors. The three sensors measures temperature, but with different working principles, the temperature data is sent to the Xively's platform in the cloud.

Thus, the information can be monitored in real time from anywhere in the world (based on the fact that the information is now available in the cloud). Once the information is stored in the cloud, the SCADA system (developed with LabView) is installed on a computer which then is in charge of downloading the data.

This information has to pass through different active network components from its source in the cloud to its destination in the SCADA system. Finally, the data is processed by the system to control the PLC action. We developed a redundant system for temperature measurement with three different type of sensor, i.e., (thermocouple, thermistor, and integrate circuit -LM35-). The system average the information gathered by the different sensor, in this way, if any of the sensors fails the system will continue up and running because the information processed by the SCADA system will be the average.

The average temperate is analyzed by the supervision system in order to take a decision based on a threshold value or set point. Once the system takes a decision, it communicates with the PLC to perform an action, in our case the action will be to open or close a cylinder according to the temperature value. The developed system allows the sensors to be placed remotely in any location in the world and to gather this information to process it in the supervision system and then performs an action with the PLC according to the values reported by the sensors.

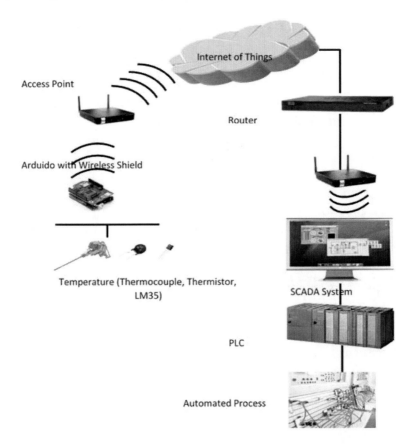

Figure 2. Real Topology.

2. MATHEMATICAL MODEL WITH PETRI NETWORKS

In this section, we will make a brief introduction to Petri Nets and then we will describe the Petri Net built to model our IWSN and the communication flow from the sensors to the SCADA system and the PLC. A Petri net was used in this work to model the sensor's network system.

Petri Nets

A Petri Net is used as a mathematical and modeling tool to describe the communication system between the sensors and the PLC in a data network. A Petri Net can be described with the following definitions [22][23]:

Definition A: A Petri Net (P/T), is a tuple $N = < P, T, Pre, Post >$ where:

- P is a finite set of places
- T is a finite set of transitions disjoint from P where $P \cap T = \emptyset$
- $Pre, Post \in N^{|P|*|T|}$ are incidence matrix of N.
- $C = Post - Pre$, is denoted as the incidence Matrix of N

There exists and arc with weight $n > 0$ from a place $p \in P$,, towards a transition $t \in T$ if and only if $Pre\ [p, t] = n\ with\ n > 0$, and, there exists an arc with weight $n > 0$ from a transition $t \in T$ towards a place $p \in P$ if and only if $Post\ [p, t] = n\ with\ n > 0$. Thus, the set of arcs from N are defined as follows:

$$F := \{(p, t) \in P.T\ /\ Pre[p, t]\} > 0\} \cup \{(t, p) \in T.P\ /Post\ [p, t] > 0\} \quad (1)$$

Consequently, there exists an alternative definition of N more suitable for the graphical representation of a Petri Net.

Definition B: A Petri Net is defined as a tuple $N = < P, T, F, W, M_0 >$ where:

- $< P, T, F >$ is a net (Definition A) with P, T finite sets and
- $W : F \rightarrow N \setminus \{0\}$ is a weight function
- $M_0 : P \rightarrow N$ is an initial mark

A mark M_0 is a vector with size $|P|$ that represents the state of the system with $M(p) = q$, i.e., there are q tokens in M in the place p.

Definition C: SWI (Sensor Wireless Industry) is a 4th-tuple $<P, T, F, W, M_0>$ where:

- $P = \{t_1, t_2, t_3, \dots \dots, t_n\}$
- $T = \{t_1, t_2, t_3, \dots \dots, t_n\}$
- $w\left(p_1, t_1\right) = 1, w\left(t_1, p_2\right), \dots w\left(p_n, t_{n-1}\right) = 1, \dots$
- $F = \{\left(p_1, t_1\right), \left(t_1, p_2\right), \dots \dots \left(p_n, t_{n-1}\right) \dots\}$

Definition D: A message in the network (P/T) from SWI N is a vector $m \in N^{|P|}$. N with a mark m_0 (initial mark) is defined as (P/T) system SWI and it is denoted by $S = < N, m_0 >$.

Petri Nets Modeling for the Sensors Network

In this work we modeled the implemented (Figure 3) IWSN by using the Petri Nets and the WoPeD (Workflow Petri Net Designer) software. WoPeD is licensed under the LGPL license. It allows to model and to analyze the control processes as well as the resources by using control flow networks (an extension of Petri Nets). In the figure 3, the token (p_1), represents the initial mark of the system. (t_1), represents the transitions with unlabeled arcs and weight $w\left(p_1, t_1\right) = 1 \dots$ The subset Sub_1, represents the wireless communication between the Arduino with wireless shield and the router. Based on a Petri Net type (P/T) the following model is built for the wireless communication in the sensors network.

According to the definition C:
Where:

$P = \{$sensors (Thermocouple, Thermistor, LM35), Arduino with Wi-Fi shield, Router, Xively, Pc/labview, PLC Siemens$\}$.

$T = \{t_1, t_2, Sub_1, t_3, Sub_4, t_4\}$

$W : F \rightarrow N \setminus \{0\}$ is a weight function defined as follows:

$$F = \{(p_1, t_1), (t_1, p_2), (t_1, p_3), (t_1, p_4), (p_2, t_2), (p_3, t_2), (p_4, t_2), (t_2, p_5), (p_5, Sub_1),$$
$$(sub_1, p_6), (p_6, t_3), (t_3, p_7), (p_7, sub_2), (sub_2, p_8), (p_8, t_4), (t_4, p_9)\} \rightarrow \text{Arcs.} \quad (2)$$

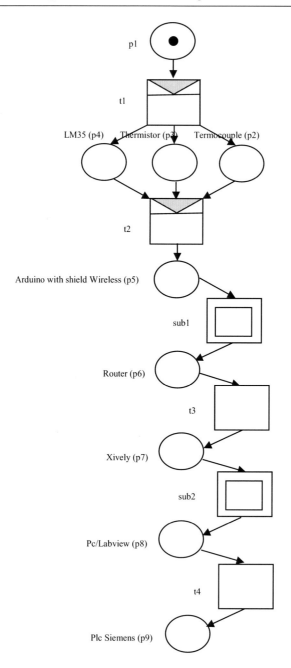

Figure 3. General Petri Net.

$$Weight = W\ (p_1, t_1) = 1, W(t_1, p_2) = 1, \ldots .. W(t_4, p_9) = 1 \qquad (3)$$

Where: p = place, t = transitions, sub = sub − processes.

Source = $p1$, Thermocouple = $p2$, Thermistor = $p3$, LM35 = $p4$, Arduino
with Wireless shield = $p5$, Router = $p6$, Xively = $p7$, PC/Labview = $p8$ and
Plc Siemens = $p9$ (4)

The complete system communication is represented in a matrix form. In
the matrix, the columns represents the transitions, the rows represents the
places and the cells the connections between them. (Refer to Table I).
$Pre, Post \in N^{|P|*|T|}$ are incidence matrixes of N, defined as in Table I and
Table II.

The previous incidence matrix is the result of the arc formed from the
places (p) to the transitions(t), i.e., $p \rightarrow t$. Initially, there exists a place $p1$ that
represents the universe of environment where the Petri Net is placed and it is
started with an arc addressed to the transition $t1$. In this case, the transition $t1$
has an input (precondition) such that when it is activated the sensors are ready
to send the information to the microcontroller. The next cycle represents the
sending of data from the three sensors $(p2, p3, p4)$ to the Arduino with
wireless shield $(p5)$, i.e., $p2, p3, p4 \rightarrow t2$ (input to $t2$).

The matrix shows the input to the transition $(t2)$ from the sensors
$(p2 = 1, p3 = 1, p4 = 1)$ which arcs have a weight function of 1. The cycle
continues until the data from the sensors is received by the PLC that performs
the final action, i.e., activate the engine according to the set point. The Table
II, describes the posterior incidence matrix. In this matrix the columns
represents the transitions, the rows represents the places and the cells the
connection between them.

The posterior incidence matrix is the result of the arc formed from
transitions (t) to the places (p), i.e., $t \rightarrow p$. Initially, there exists a transition
$t1$ that represents the event of changing from the initial place $p1$ to the places
$p2, p3, p4$ (the three sensors). In this case the transition $t1$ has three output
arcs (post conditional) such that when it is activated the sensors are ready to
send the information to the microcontroller.

Table I. Previous Incidence Matrix

Pre	t1	t2	sub1	t3	sub2	t4
p1	1	0	0	0	0	0
p2	0	1	0	0	0	0
p3	0	1	0	0	0	0
p4	0	1	0	0	0	0
p5	0	0	1	0	0	0
p6	0	0	0	1	0	0
p7	0	0	0	0	1	0
p8	0	0	0	0	0	1
p9	0	0	0	0	0	0

Table II. Posterior Incidence Matrix

Post	t1	t2	sub1	t3	sub2	t4
p1	0	0	0	0	0	0
p2	1	0	0	0	0	0
p3	1	0	0	0	0	0
p4	1	0	0	0	0	0
p5	0	1	0	0	0	0
p6	0	0	1	0	0	0
p7	0	0	0	1	0	0
p8	0	0	0	0	1	0
p9	0	0	0	0	0	1

The cycle represents the sending of data from the three sensors $(p2, p3, p4)$ to the Arduino with wireless shield $(p5)$, i.e., $t2 \rightarrow p5$ ($t2$ output). The matrix shows the output from the transition $t1$ to the sensors $(p2 = 1, p3 = 1, p4 = 1)$ which arcs have a mark or weight equal to 1. The cycle continues until the data from the sensor is received by the PLC that performs the action, i.e., activate the engine according to the set point. The incidence matrix, is the result of subtracting the matrixes post and pre, i.e., $C = Post - Pre$. Consequently, the post matrix pair $(p1, t1 = 0)$ and the pre matrix pair $(p1, t1 = 1) \rightarrow 0 - 1 = -1$ (incidence matrix pair $(p1, t1)$ and so on until the matrix is complete (Refer to Table III).

The matrix shows that the complete network is unidirectional and consequently $p1$ has only one direction to $t1$ but not in the opposite direction (-1).

Additionally, the incidence matrix allows the places and transitions to determine the arcs that they are connected to and to obtain information about them, for instance to be able to determine the inputs and outputs in a transition. Finally, it is convenient to define marks as vectors which their inputs are defined as integers (assuming that the places forms a set completely ordered). The initial mark in (P/T) IWN in the vector $M_0 = (1,0,0,0,0,0,0,0,0)$. and the cycle continues until completing the occurrences sequence shown in Table IV.

Table III. Incidence Matrix $C = Post - Pre$

Post	$t1$	$t2$	$sub1$	$t3$	$sub2$	$t4$
$p1$	-1	0	0	0	0	0
$p2$	1	-1	0	0	0	0
$p3$	1	-1	0	0	0	0
$p4$	1	-1	0	0	0	0
$p5$	0	1	-1	0	0	0
$p6$	0	0	1	-1	0	0
$p7$	0	0	0	1	-1	0
$p8$	0	0	0	0	1	-1
$p9$	0	0	0	0	0	1

Table IV. Secuence of Ocurrences (M_0)

$$
\begin{bmatrix} 1 \\ 0 \\ 0 \\ 0 \\ 0 \\ 0 \\ 0 \\ 0 \\ 0 \end{bmatrix}
\xrightarrow{t1}
\begin{bmatrix} 0 \\ 1 \\ 1 \\ 1 \\ 0 \\ 0 \\ 0 \\ 0 \\ 0 \end{bmatrix}
\xrightarrow{t2}
\begin{bmatrix} 0 \\ 0 \\ 0 \\ 0 \\ 1 \\ 0 \\ 0 \\ 0 \\ 0 \end{bmatrix}
\xrightarrow{s1}
\begin{bmatrix} 0 \\ 0 \\ 0 \\ 0 \\ 0 \\ 1 \\ 0 \\ 0 \\ 0 \end{bmatrix}
\xrightarrow{t3}
\begin{bmatrix} 0 \\ 0 \\ 0 \\ 0 \\ 0 \\ 0 \\ 1 \\ 0 \\ 0 \end{bmatrix}
\xrightarrow{s2}
\begin{bmatrix} 0 \\ 0 \\ 0 \\ 0 \\ 0 \\ 0 \\ 0 \\ 1 \\ 0 \end{bmatrix}
\xrightarrow{t4}
\begin{bmatrix} 0 \\ 0 \\ 0 \\ 0 \\ 0 \\ 0 \\ 0 \\ 0 \\ 1 \end{bmatrix}
$$

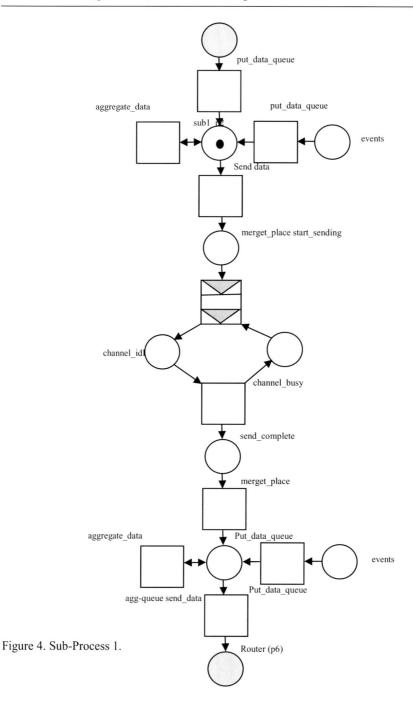

Figure 4. Sub-Process 1.

In other words, when an enabled transition is triggered, it will change the distribution of the signals (marks). In this way, a trigger sequence will produce a marking sequence and consequently the Table IV is formed:

Mathematical Model for Sub-Process 1

The mathematical model for the sub-process 1 is defined as follows (Figure 4).
Where:

$$P = \{\text{Arduino with Wi-Fi shield, sub1\_}p2\text{, events, merged place,}$$
$$\text{channel\_idle, channel, channel busy, agg-queue, Router}\}. \tag{5}$$

$$T = \{\text{put\_data\_queue, aggregate data, send data, star\_sending}\}. \tag{6}$$

F = {(Arduino with shield Wi-Fi, pit_data_queue), (put_data queue, sub1_p2), (put_data queue,sub1_p2),(sub1_p2,aggregate data), (aggregate data, sub1_p2), (events, put_data queue), (put_data queue, sub1_p2), (sub1_p2,send data), (send data, merged_place), (merged_place, star sending), (star_sending, channel_idle), (channel_idle, send complete), (send complete, channel busy), (channel busy, star sending), (star sending, channel_idle), (channel_idle, send complete), (send complete, merged place), (merged place, put_data queue), (put_data queue, agg_queue), (events, put_data queue), (put_data queue, agg_queue), (agg_queue, send_data), (send_data, Router)}.
(7)

$$W = \{\text{(Arduino with shield Wi-Fi, put\_data queue)}$$
$$= 1,...., \text{(agg\_queue, send\_data)} = 1\} \tag{8}$$

Mathematical Model for Sub-Process 2

The sub-process 2 in the Petri Net (Figure 5) represents the medium access control in the Ethernet technology and it is modeled as follows:

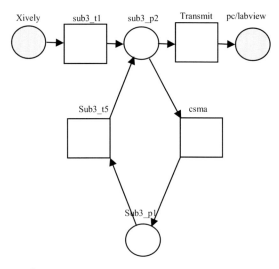

Figure 5. Sub-Process 2.

Where:

$$P = \{Xively, sub3\_p2, sub3\_p1, pc/Labview\} \qquad (9)$$

$$T = \{sub3\_t1, sub3\_t5, csma, transmit\} \qquad (10)$$

F = {(Xively, sub3_t1), (sub3_t1, sub3_p2), (sub3_p2,csma), (csma, sub3_p1), (sub3_p1, sub3_t5), (sub3_t5, sub3_p2), (sub3_p2, transmit), (transmit, pc/labview)}.

$$W = \{(Xively, sub3\_t1) = 1,...,(trasmit, pc/labview) = 1 \qquad (11)$$

3. NETWORK COMMUNICATION AND DATA FLOW ANALYSIS

In this section we will show a network analysis performed in the IWSN. In this analysis we measured different network parameters in the path from the source nodes (sensors) to the destination (cloud system – Xively).

In the first part we measure all the hops involved in the routing path from the sensors the Xively's web portal. In order to do this, we use the tool Patchar. This program measures performance metrics in data networks. The tool sends multiple packets with 45 different sizes in the range from 64 to 1500 bytes (1500 bytes is the MTU in the localhost). Additionally, the program uses 32 sets of packets per hop. Thus, a total of 11.520 packets are send over the network. The results are average as shown below and the result of the total measurement is shown in Table V:

root@felipe-MS-7636:/home/felipe#./pathchar 216.52.233.121
pathchar to 216.52.233.121 (216.52.233.121)
can't find path mtu - using 1500 bytes.
doing 32 probes at each of 45 sizes (64 to 1500 by 32)
0 192.168.0.3 (192.168.0.3)
| 39 Mb/s, 124 us (557 us)
1 192.168.0.1 (192.168.0.1)
| 722 Kb/s, 14.8 ms (46.7 ms), 11% dropped
10.32.0.26 (10.32.0.26)

Table V. Traffic Measures

Link	Host	IP	BW	Latency	Drodped	Queuing
0	Arduino with Wireless Shield	192.168.0.3	39 Mb/s	124 µs		
1	Access Point	192.168.0.1	722 Kb/s	14.8 ms	11%	
2		10.32.0.26				
3		*201.244.1.150				
		*10.5.4.70				
		*201.244.1.5		490µs		
4	sta.etb.net.co	10.5.4.74		27ms		
5	Edge3.Miami1	4.59.82.113				
		*4.69.138.77		73 µs	42%	
6	Edge2.Miami2	4.69.138.109	571Mb/s	345 µs		1.23 ms
7	globalcrossing	4.68.111.122	178 Mb/s	156 µs		
8	ae9.scr4.gblx.net	67.16.147.129		30.1 ms		
9	po2.gblx.net	67.17.95.214		161 ms		
10	INTERNAP	64.215.30.78				
		*216.52.255.46	49 Mb/s	4 µs		1.55ms
11	pnap.net	216.52.255.110		135 ms		
12	Logmein.net (Xively)	63.251.195.114				
*		210.52.233.121				

In the above table it is possible to see the bandwidth available in the different hosts involved in the communications. Likewise, it is possible to see the hop-to-hop latency and packet lost ratio. As shown in the table, the internet has multiple devices with different qualities in the channels. Specifically, there is a hop (4.69.138.77) with 42% of drop packets.

Consequently, our application sends the information gathered from the sensors over the HTTP protocol. It uses TCP in the transport layer of the OSI model. TCP can handles packet loss by keeping track of the connection. In this way, any packet loss can be retransmitted avoiding loss of information and because the amount of bandwidth involved in the transmission is minimum due to the data sent within the packets this is a good approach to implement. Furthermore, we measure the RTT (Round Trip Time) with two different protocols, i.e., ICMP and HTTP. We implemented the tool SmokePing[1] and performed the test during 30 hours to obtain trustable results (the results are average over a huge sample size). The tool calculates the RTT according following equation (12)[24]:

$$RRT = \left(delay + \left(\frac{packt_{size}}{Bandwitdh}\right)\right) + delay \tag{12}$$

The Figure 6 shows the results obtained from the SmokePing tool after the 30 hours of measurement with the ICMP protocol to the Xively web platform. According to the results the maximum packet loss average is 3.39% and the average RTT is 161.7ms with a 28.7 ms standard deviation. These values represents a good quality in the channels based on the amount of data send with the information from the sensors (very low bandwidth demanding) and the connection oriented protocol used by the HTTP put method.

The second method used to measure the latency in the communication (RTT) is by sending HTTP packets. The same tool SmokePing was implemented. As explained before, we measure the HTTP RTT because the protocol used to send the information gathered from the sensors is HTTP. This protocol is reliable due to the transport protocol used according to the OSI model, i.e., TCP. The Figure 7 shows the results obtained, i.e., round trip time in the communication from the source nodes (sensors) and the Xively's web-portal in the Internet (Public IP address 216.52.233.21). The results show the average RTT to be 177.7 ms with a 6.1 ms standard deviation.

---

[1] SmokePing is a deluxe latency measurement tool. It can measure, store and display latency, latency distribution and packet loss. SmokePing uses RRDtool to maintain a longterm data-store and to draw pretty graphs, giving up to the minute information on the state of each network connection.

In the Figure 8, we analyse the packets send by the Arduino that contains the temperature values. As stated before, the information is sent through the HTTP protocol and specifically the PUT method. This method sends the information to a web server (api.xively.com) [26] that is constantly listening to the connection initialized by the client, in this case the Arduino.

The body of the packet shows the information send to the web server located in the cloud. In this case, it is possible to see the values of the three different sensors, in the following format:

"Sensor_reading", "current_value":21.15
"Sensor_reading2", "current_value":17.62
"Sensor_reading3", "current_value":9.04

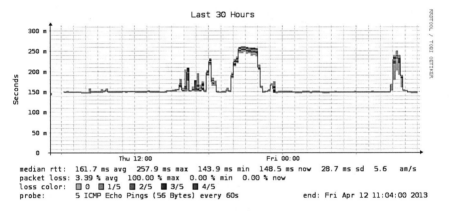

Figure 6. RTT in Xively Simulated with SmokePing.

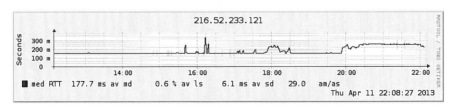

Figure 7. RTT in HTTP Simulated in SmokePing.

```
⊟ Hypertext Transfer Protocol
  ⊟ PUT /v2/feeds/75924.json HTTP/1.1\r\n
    ⊟ [Expert Info (Chat/Sequence): PUT /v2/feeds/75924.json HTTP/1.1\r\n]
        [Message: PUT /v2/feeds/75924.json HTTP/1.1\r\n]
        [Severity level: Chat]
        [Group: Sequence]
      Request Method: PUT
      Request URI: /v2/feeds/75924.json
      Request Version: HTTP/1.1
    Host: api.cosm.com\r\n
    User-Agent: Arduino/2.0\r\n
    X-ApiKey: CTqSu_Oy82CqqGPcEp7NwPG2v6eSAKxzS0FuTnc4YzE5Yz0g\r\n
  ⊟ Content-Length: 220\r\n
      [Content length: 220]
    \r\n
    [Full request URI: http://api.cosm.com/v2/feeds/75924.json]
  ⊟ Data (220 bytes)
      Data: 7b0d0a2276657273696f6e223a22312e302e30222c0d0a22...
      [Length: 220]
```

```
00d0  69 64 22 20 3a 20 22 73  65 6e 73 6f 72 5f 72 65    id" : "s ensor_re
00e0  61 64 69 6e 67 22 2c 20  22 63 75 72 72 65 6e 74    ading", "current
00f0  5f 76 61 6c 75 65 22 20  3a 20 22 32 31 2e 31 35    _value" : "21.15
0100  22 20 7d 2c 0d 0a 7b 20  22 69 64 22 20 3a 20 22    " },..{ "id" : "
0110  73 65 6e 73 6f 72 5f 72  65 61 64 69 6e 67 32 22    sensor_r eading2"
0120  2c 20 22 63 75 72 72 65  6e 74 5f 76 61 6c 75 65    , "curre nt_value
0130  22 20 3a 20 22 31 37 2e  36 32 22 20 7d 2c 0d 0a    " : "17. 62" },..
0140  7b 20 22 69 64 22 20 3a  20 22 73 65 6e 73 6f 72    { "id" : "sensor
0150  5f 72 65 61 64 69 6e 67  33 22 2c 20 22 63 75 72    _reading 3", "cur
0160  72 65 6e 74 5f 76 61 6c  75 65 22 20 3a 20 22 31    rent_val ue" : "1
0170  39 2e 30 34 22 20 7d 0d  0a 5d 0d 0a 7d 0d 0a       9.04" }. .]..}..
```

Figure 8. HTTP Protocol.

We also analyzed the TCP connection. Thus, the figure 9 shows the TCP flow created in an established session from the sensors to the cloud web server. In this figure it is possible to see how the "three way handshake" process is initialized from the private network host 192.168.0.3 to the public server 216.52.233.121. The sync packets starts the conversation in the client/server architecture and then a series of ACK packets are sent to the client to confirm the reception of the information coming from the sensors. This way, it is possible to track the connection and to warranty the arrival of the packet and consequently to avoid loss of information.

Finally, the TCP flow is plotted as shown in the Figure 10. In this figure, it is possible to see as black impulses the packets corresponding to the TCP source port and as red points the packets corresponding to the TCP destination port. The acknowledgements are shown with green bars and the sync packets with black lines.

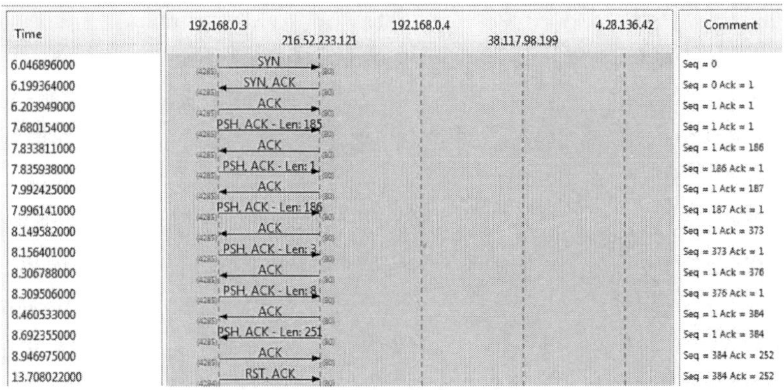

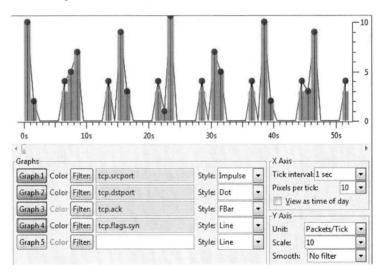

Figure 9. TCP Negotiation.

Figure 10. TCP Sequence.

4. APPLIED INTERNET OF THINGS

The Xively's platform allows to capture the data from the sensor through the internet [25] in real time and gives a suite of possibilities with the information gathered, such as: creation of graphs, alerts and access to historical data. The platform is special for the visualization of the information sent by the sensors connected to the Arduino. The platform allows to receive the data by using a model based on feeds and data streams. The feed represents the location where the data is generated and a data stream represents the sensors (individually) associated to this location, e.g., temperature sensor, gas sensors and so on.

It is possible to manually create a feed to simulate the data sending as follows:

curl --request POST \
--data '{"Temperature":"75924", "version":"1.0.0"}' \
--header "X-ApiKey: CTqSu_Oy82CqqGPcEp7NwPG2v6e SAKxzS0 FuTnc4 YzE5Yz0g"
--verbose \ http://api.xively.com/v2/feeds.

The X-ApiKey value is generated by the Xively's platform as a way to identify a unique process. The sensors can be monitored from anywhere in the world without changing the network configuration even if the sensors are moved among different locations. The figure 11 shows the graphs created with the information and the possibility to zoom in the graphs to visualize historical data.

The figure 12 shows the location of the sensors sending the information to the cloud platform according to the feed ID, thus you can easily locate the sensors.

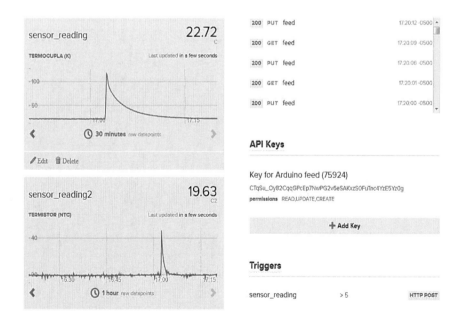

Figure 11. Temperature Graph Xively.

Figure 12. Location Sensors.

5. SCADA SYSTEM

We implemented a SCADA system with the LabView programming language. This system communicates with the Internet and downloads the data gathered by the sensors. The SCADA system is installed in a PC with internet access. The developed system is able to process the information and then send it to the PLC by using the OPC standard. Thus, the PLC is able to perform the action sent by the SCADA system. Figure 13 shows both the Wireshark capture in the SCADA site and the web-platform output. It shows the put and get method which allows the information to be gathered from the sensors (192.168.0.3) and sent to the supervision system. The 200 code means a confirmation of the operation (upload or download).

Based on the graphical features of the LabView language we designed and coded a GUI to be able to control and plot the information gathered from the cloud. The following diagram (Figure 14) shows the general communication flow beneath the SCADA system. In this diagram we depict graphically the programming used for the design of the supervision system and the communications steps involved.

As stated before, the communication protocol used to connect the supervision system and the PLC is OPC (OLE for Process Control) [27]. This protocol is a communication interface to interconnect control and supervision devices from multiple vendors. Thus, the communication is normalized and the system is able to connect to multiple devices such as PLC, RTU (Remote Terminal Units) or sensors. The communication model in OPC is based on the server/client architecture. There is one server and multiple clients connecting the server for reading or writing a variable.

The Figure 15 show the GUI developed for our SCADA system. It allows to control and supervise the industrial process. In this case the temperature monitoring. The figure shows the relation between the SCADA system and the Siemens PLC. Start and Stop (E4.0, E4.1) are physical inputs in the PLC for the manual management mode. In the automatic mode Start LV and Stop LV represents the virtual inputs that will perform the action sent by the supervision system according to the set point, i.e., if the temperature is over the set point value the engine is activated.

6. PETRI NET SIMULATION AND RESULTS

In a Petri Net (type $(^P/_T)$ in our work) is very important the system to have the following features: boundedness, liveness, deadlock, reversibility. Thus, the proposed system shown in the section "MATHEMATICAL MODEL WITH PETRI NETWORKS" was simulated with WOPED (Work Petri Net Designer) to check the properties mentioned before. The Figure 16 shows that the simulated model fulfills all the features and consequently corresponds to a robust model that represents correctly the real sensor's network. In order to analyze the proposed Petri Net the enumeration method was used.

This method is based on a graph construction, called "Coverability Graph". The graph represents each mark vector in the net and the transitions among them. The figure 17 shows the coverability graph for the proposed Petri Net. As depicted in the figure, there exists multiple nodes with binary sequences connected through the transitions defined in the proposed Petri Net. The occurrences sequence (refer to Table IV) is one of the possibilities of the coverability graph.

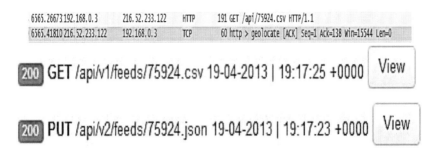

Figure 13. Methods Get and Put in Xively.

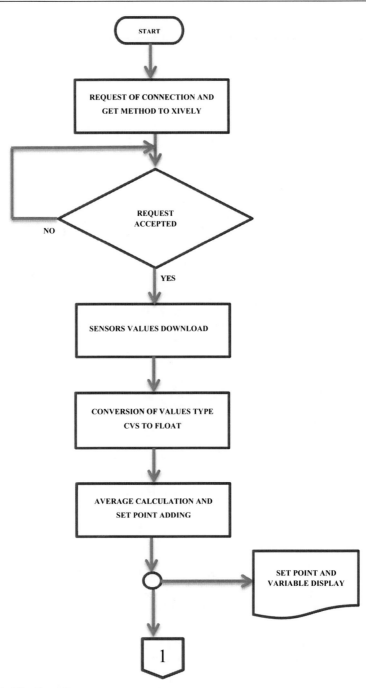

Figure 14. (Continued).

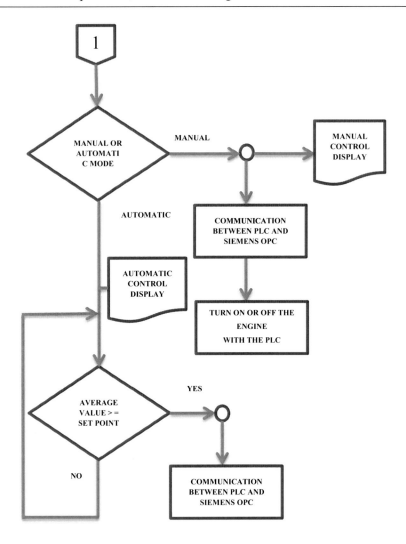

Figure 14. Labview Programming.

Furthermore, based on the fact that the mathematical model for the proposed Petri Net corresponds to a workflow, it was possible to perform a dynamical analysis through the simulation of the sensor's network. The analysis is based on the results obtained with the SmokePing tool (where the average RTT was found). Consequently, the RTT was set as a continuous variable in the simulation, please refer to Figure 18.

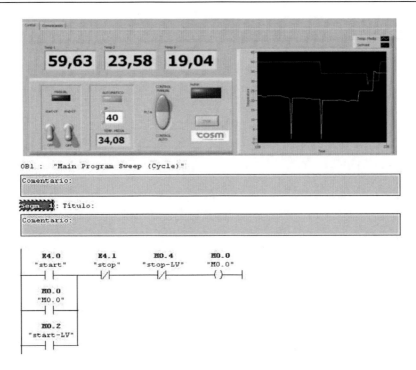

Figure 15. Control of the System.

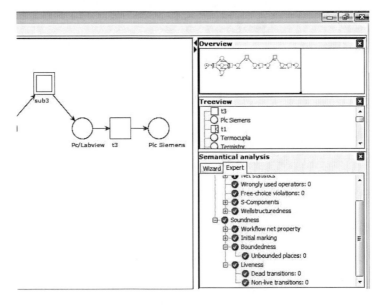

Figure 16. Desirable Properties Petri Net.

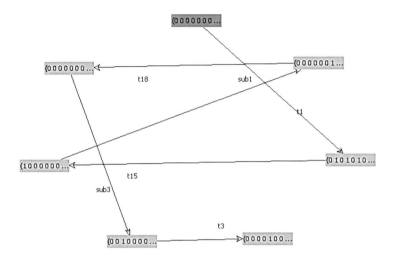

Figure 17. Coverability Graph.

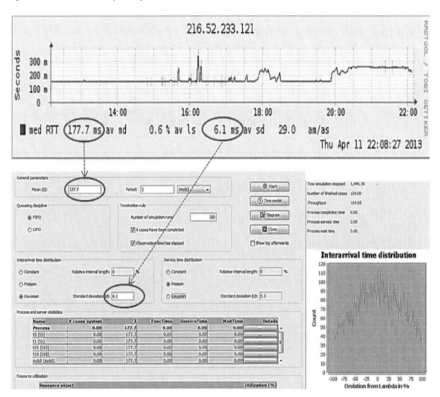

Figure 18. Real RTT (Day 1).

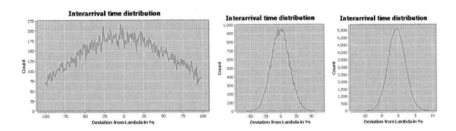

Figure 19. Gaussian pattern (Deviation from Lambda λ in %) Day 5, 10 y 30.

The simulation's results (performed in the WOPED software) describe the behavior of the Petri net to follow a statistical pattern that starts in a chaotic state in the first day (refer to Figure 18) and improves to a better state in the 5th day, then, in the 10th day the system exhibits a more stable behavior that follows a Gaussian pattern. Thus, indicating that the system follows a dynamic flow of information in terms of the RTT time inserted to simulate the model. Consequently, the output values in the simulation are close to the average (λ) obtained with the SmokePing software in the real life. The stabilization of the system is based on the fact that with the pass of the days the simulation obtains more samples and consequently the state of the variable RTT becomes more stable. Therefore, in the 30th simulation day the results depicts a perfect defined Gaussian pattern (Refer to figure 19). This indicates the final stabilization of the IWSN and consequently the network is ready to be used. In an IP network the RTT can be a random value because it is not possible to control all the devices and channels (queuing, band width, QoS) in the path from the source nodes to their destination, in our case the sensors and the supervision system. But according to the simulated Petri Net model the results shows that even though the RTT can have multiple values the communication is still possible. After that, it is necessary to analyze specific requirements in the maximum acceptable communication delay but that is something that depends on the services being monitored. In our case, the communication process from the sensors to the execution of the action in the PLC takes around 10 to 15 seconds, but this is because of a restriction in the Xyvely's cloud platform. They have a security policy where a certain maximum rate of packets is allowed in order to avoid congestion and saturation in the platform. This is mainly because they accept traffic from all the world. Consequently, this additional delay is reflected in the developed system. Thus, the current system is not suitable for near real time applications but this could be easily solved by changing the cloud platform.

CONCLUSION

In this work we developed an IWSN for remote monitoring and remote data acquisition. The developed IWSN is a modern and trendy system that suits the actual trends in the automation industry which tends to implement remote monitoring and control systems for industrial networks based on the IP protocol.

Thus, allowing the monitoring platform to be in the cloud and consequently to be able to monitor sensors distributed across the world. The implemented system uses temperature sensors based on the fact that this kind of sensor is highly implemented in industrial environments. It is important to note that their performance depends on the selection of the sensors according to the temperatures process to be measure. For instance, it is possible to say that the thermocouples has a main advantage over the thermistors because of their measure range, the output accuracy and the stability in the measurement. In the same way, the thermistor presents a high advantage in the sensibility to temperature changes. Thus, they are very suitable for situations where the measurement range is small and the response time is short. Oppositely, the temperature sensor based on integrated circuits are not commonly used in industrial applications but their size is perfect to be used in electronic circuits.

The wireless technology is implemented for sending the data gathered by the sensors. This is because recently the industrial networks are implementing this technology with wireless protocols such as WiFi or Zigbee in order to be able to control and monitor places with difficult access and to avoid complex wired installations. In the same way, the wireless technology presents some disadvantages such as the possibility to introduce information or packet in the middle of the communication. This is because these technologies uses the range of free frequencies. Additionally, because everybody is allowed to use this frequency ranges there will be a great electromagnetic interference which can affect the communication quality and produce possible loss of information.

The proposed system was mathematically modeled according to the Petri nets and it was simulated. The results of the simulation showed the system to be stable and reliable based on the fact that the pattern depicted in the simulation showed most of the values to fall in the average RTT taken from the measurements performed in the real network. The current system is not suitable for near real time processes because the average time to gather the data and perform an action from the SCADA system to the PLC is around 10 to 15 second. But, this is because of the restrictions of the Xyvely's platform and this could be easily overcome with the design of a cloud platform that allows a higher packet rate.

The system could be improved with further work in the following aspects:

- UDT protocol implementation as the transport protocol instead of TCP. The UDT protocol combines the reliability of TCP with the performance of UDP. It is possible to achieve a transfer rate of 9.2 Gb/s in a 10 Gb/s connection [28].
- Implementation of the 802.11n Wi-Fi protocol for faster transmission of the information.
- The implementation of IPv6 to be able to assign a unique IP address per sensor and to use native security protocols such as IPsec

REFERENCES

[1]   Chee-Yee, Chong; Kumar, S. P. *"Sensor networks: evolution, opportunities, and challenges,"* vol., 91, no.8, pp.1247-1256, Aug. 2003. doi:10.1109/JPROC.2003.814918.

[2]   Petersen, S.; Doyle, P.; Vatland, S.; Aasland, C. S.; Andersen, T. M. Dag Sjong, *"Requirements, drivers and analysis of wireless sensor network solutions for the Oil and Gasindustry,"* vol., no., pp. 219-226,25-28 Sept.2007doi: 10.1109/EFTA.2007.4416773.

[3]   Zhang, Ke; Li, Yang; Xliao, Wang-hui; Suh, Heejong. *"The Application of a Wireless Sensor Network Design Based on ZigBee in Petrochemical Industry Field,"* pp. 284-287, 1-3 Nov. doi:200810.1109/ ICINIS. 2008. 184.

[4]   Liqun, Hou; Bergmann, N. W. *"Novel Industrial Wireless Sensor Networks for Machine Condition Monitoring and Fault Diagnosis,"* vol.61, no.10, pp.2787-2798,Oct.2012 doi: 10.1109/TIM.2012.2200817.

[5]   Cena, G.; Valenzano, A.; Vitturi, S. *"Wireless extensions of wired industrial communications networks,"* 273–278. doi: 10.1109/ INDIN. 2007.4384768.

[6]   Koumpis, K.; Hanna, L.; Andersson, M.; Johansson, M. "Wireless industrial control and monitoring beyond cable replacement," in Proc. 2nd PROFIBUS Int. Conf., Coombe Abbey, Warwickshire, UK, 2005.

[7]   Hodge, V. J.; O'Keefe, S.; Weeks, M.; Moulds, A. *"Wireless Sensor Networks for Condition Monitoring in the Railway Industry: A Survey,"*

vol., 16, no.3, pp. 1088-1106, June 2015. doi: 10.1109/ TITS. 2014. 2366512.

[8]   Long, Zhaohua; Gao, Mingjun. *"Design of Wireless Sensor Networks Gateway Node and Its Industry Application,"* p.1-4, 19-20, Dec. 2009_ 10. 1109/ICIECS.2009.5366256.

[9]   San Martín, César; Torres, Flavio; Barrientos, Rodrigo. "Monitoreo y control de temperatura de un estanque de agua entre Chile y España usando redes de alta velocidad." *Revista facultad de iIngeniería, U.T.A.*, vol. 11, no. 1, pp. 41-46, julio 2003 ("Monitoring and control of temperature of a pool of water between Chile and Spain using high-speed networks." IIngeniería faculty Magazine, UTA, vol. 11, no. 1 pp. 41-46 July 2003). Accessed February 25, 2012. http://www.redalyc.org/articulo.oa?id=11411205.

[10]   Gungor, V. C.; Hancke, G. P. *"Industrial Wireless Sensor Networks: Challenges, Design Principles, and Technical Approaches,"* *vol.*, 56, no. 10, pp. 4258-4265, Oct. 2009 doi: 10.1109/TIE.2009.2015754.

[11]   Gallardo, M.; Montero, M.; Hernando, J. M.; Fontan, F. P.; Espinosa, J.; Gomez, J. I.; Hidalgo, I. *"Future tendencies in factory environment radiocommunications,"* vol., no., pp. 157-164,1997, doi: 10.1109/ WFCS.1997.

[12]   Guest Editorial Special Section on Wireless Technologies in Factory and Industrial Automation—Part II. Guest Editorial Special Section on Wireless Technologies in Factory and Industrial Automation—Part II, Miorandi, D.; Uhlemann, E.; Vitturi, S.; Willig, A.; pp. 189 - 190, DOI: 10.1109/TII.2007.903227.

[13]   Lee, J-S; Hsu, P-L. "An improved evaluation of ladder logic diagrams and petri nets for the sequence controller design in manufacturing systems," *The International Journal of Advanced Manufacturing Technology*, vol., 24, no. 3-4, pp. 279–287, 2004. [Online]. Available: http://dx.doi.org/10.1007/s00170-003-1722-y.

[14]   Zurawski, R.; Meng Chu, Zhou. "Petri nets and industrial applications: A tutorial," in *Industrial Electronics, IEEE Transactions on*, vol., 41, no.6, pp. 567-583, Dec 1994 doi: 10.1109/41.334574.

[15]   Gomes, L; Costa, A; Barros, J. P.; Pais, R.; Rodrigues, T.; Ferreira, R. *"Petri Net based Building Automation and Monitoring System,"* vol., 1, no., pp. 57-62, 23-27 June 2007 doi: 10.1109/INDIN.2007.4384731.

[16]   Xiao, Fu; Zhiqiang, Ma; Zhenhua, Yu; Gang, Fu. *"On Wireless Sensor Networks Formal Modeling Based on Petri Nets,"* vol., no., pp.1-4, 23-25 Sept. 2011 doi: 10.1109/wicom.2011.6040356.

[17] Nastic, S.; Sehic, S.; Duc-Hung, Le; Hong-Linh, Truong; Dustdar, S. *"Provisioning Software-Defined IoT Cloud Systems,"* vol., no., pp. 288-295, 27-29 Aug. 2014, doi: 10.1109/FiCloud.2014.52.

[18] Yinghui, Huang; Guanyu, Li. *"Descriptive models for Internet of Things,"* vol., no., pp. 483-486, 13-15Aug.2010, doi: 10.1109/ ICICIP. 2010.5564232.

[19] Qian, Zhu; Ruicong, Wang; Qi, Chen; Yan, Liu; Weijun, Qin. *"IOT Gateway: Bridging Wireless Sensor Networks into Internet of Things,"* vol., no., pp. 347-352, 11-13 Dec. 2010, doi: 10.1109/EUC.2010.58.

[20] Hui, Suo; Jiafu, Wan; Caifeng, Zou; Jianqi, Liu. *"Security in the Internet of Things: A Review,"* vol., 3, no., pp. 648-651, 23-25March, 2012, doi: 10.1109/ICCSEE.2012.373.

[21] Gupta, R.; Garg, R. *"Mobile Applications Modelling and Security Handling in Cloud-Centric Internet of Things,"* vol., no., pp. 285-290, 1-2May2015, doi:101109-015.119.

[22] Fu, X.; Ma, Z.; Yu, Z.; Fu, G. "On wireless sensor networks formal modeling based on petri nets," in Proceedings of the 7th International Conference on Wireless Communications, Networking and Mobile Computing (WiCOM '11), pp. 1–4, 2011. http:// www.oalib.com/ references/13815795.

[23] Cervantes, J. *"Representacion y aprendizaje de conocimiento con redes de petri difusas,"* 2005 ("Knowledge representation and learning fuzzy Petri nets," 2005). http:// www.ctrl.cinvestav.mx/ ~yuw/ pdf/ MaTesCCJ.pdf.

[24] Mnisi, N. V.; Oyedapo, O. J.; Kurien, A. *"Active Throughput Estimation Using RTT of Differing ICMP Packet Sizes,"* vol., no., pp.480-485, 23-26 Nov. 2008 doi: 10.1109/BROADCOM.2008.76.

[25] Sinha, N.; Pujitha, K. E.; Alex, J. S. R. *"Xively based sensing and monitoring system for IoT,"* vol., no., pp.1-6, 8-10 Jan. 2015 doi: 10.1109/ ICCCI. 2015.721814.

[26] Corso, F.; Camargo, Y.; Ramirez, L. *"Wireless Sensor System According to the Concept of IoT -Internet of Things-"*, pp.52,58, 10-13 March 2014, doi: 10.1109/CSCI.2014.17.

[27] Lakshmi, A.; Sangeetha, B.; Naveenkumar, A.; Ganesh, B.; Bharathi, N. *"Experimental validation of PID based cascade control system through SCADA-PLC-OPC interface,"* pp.1-4, 10-12 Jan. 2012. doi: 10.1109/ ICCCI.2012.6158893.

[28] Bernardo, D. V.; Doan, Hoang. *"Network security considerations for a new generation protocol UDT,"* pp.125-130, 8-11 Aug. 2009 doi: 10. 1109/ICCSIT.2009.5234768.

[29] Bruno Lacerda and Pedro U. Lima, "Petri Nets as an Analysis Tool For Data Flow in," https://www.cs.bham.ac.uk/~lacerdab/papers/sn.pdf.

In: The Internet of Things (IoT)　　　ISBN: 978-1-63484-626-4
Editor: Silvia Watts　　　© 2016 Nova Science Publishers, Inc.

Chapter 3

THE IMPORTANCE OF INTERNET OF THINGS GOVERNANCE: A PUBLIC-PRIVATE PARTNERSHIPS FOR TECHNICAL COOPERATION

*Analía Aspis**

University of Buenos Aires
Law Research Institute Ambrosio Gioja
Buenos Aires, Argentina

ABSTRACT

The article presents the current debate related to Internet of Things governance, its main challenges and the importance of public- private partnerships for technical cooperation.

INTRODUCTION

The proliferation of devices with the ability to communicate and transmit information to each other is the basis of the dynamics of Internet of Things (IoT), enabling new communication capabilities, data processing and access to

---
* E-mail address: analia.aspis@gmail.com.

information. Perceived as a means to generate both social and economic impacts among the information society, IoT defy the current Internet Governance framework and the role of the public sector. Accordingly, this paper aims to present the current IoT governance scenario, its main challenges, the role of the governments and the need to develop public-private partnerships for technical cooperation in the governance of IoT resources.

1. INTERNET OF THINGS ERA

The term IoT was first defined by Kevin Ashton in 1998 [1] who described it as an architecture capable of information management on a global network. Subsequently, the Advisory Group of the European Union Program on Information Society Technologies referred to IoT as an ambient intelligence where people can interact intelligently and intuitively through everyday objects. Hence, IoT is presented as a network where people, objects and the environment are interconnected by interfaces that connect and communicate things and individuals [4]. Accordingly, the International Telecommunication Union (ITU) described IoT as a *global infrastructure* for the *Information Society* that fosters the delivery of advanced information and communications services through the interconnection of objects [5].

Consequently, the dawning of the age of IoT, sometimes also referred to as the Internet of Everything (IoE), includes the interoperability of information and communications technology from innumerable locations and situations. This allows a wide range of scoping and analytical possibilities such as logistics information, location of items, instrumentation streams to and from devices, remote and automated data collection, processes automation and immediate capability to act remotely on real-world environments.

2. IoT ARCHITECTURE

Regarding the taxonomy of this new type of connection between or through physical objects, we can identify certain elements that the literature mentions as technically required to manage an IoT ecosystem such as:

Hardware. Devices. Types of devices. IoT devices collect information from different types of networks to provide information for further processing [6] and some devices also perform processing operations based on information received from other objects. IoT network includes many types of mechanisms such as acquisition, detection and data drive devices, geolocation technologies such as radio frequency, infrared systems, optical, sensors, actuators and other communication hardware.

Methods for object identification. Electronic Product Code and the Uniform Code Council. The objects of IoT are uniquely identified either by labels, tags, sensors or other electronic devices. Since 2003 EPCglobal, a non-profit organization resulting from the merger of the European Article Number (EAN) and the Uniform Code Council (UCC), has regulated and managed the Global Trade Item Number (GTIN), which provides a unique identification to every single product. Furthermore, EPCglobal has awarded a contract to Verisign to maintain the root directory object name service, which allows the redirection of the stored or readable information in the labels or middleware backend. EPCglobal is managed by a Board of Governors, in which different industrial sectors are represented by global corporations from Europe, North America, Japan and China.[2]

Communication and identification services. Object name service. The object name service (ONS) is an automated service network similar to the domain name service (DNS)[3] which allows communication between different devices within a single or multiple network [7]. When an interrogator device (for example, a radio frequency reader) reads a label, this information is transmitted to an ONS[4] - located in a private network or the Internet - to find information on that product. It should be noted that to date there is no uniformity regarding the management of ONS and therefore a fragmented IoT scenario, where different protocols, standards and routing system may arise. For example, Verisign, Afilias[5] and GS1[6] are providers who have started their services, too closely with the private sector.

---

[2] The public sector is represented by the United States Department leading to criticism from some of parties who fear a strong influence by the US government. This issue has been discussed several times in Europe, for critical positions on the management of EPCglobal.

[3] For similarities and differences between the ONS system and DNS see Weber, Rolf. 2009. "Internet of things - Need for a new legal environment", Computer Law & Security Review, Elsevier, p. 523, accessed 10. November, 2015 at http://www.researchgate.net/publication/222544977_Internet_of_thing__Need_for_a_new_legal_environment.

[4] The ONS serves as a directory for EPC numbers and is used by companies who want to know details of another company where they may not have a previously established relationship.

[5] Afilias is a global provider of domain name registration of Internet based in Dublin, Ireland. The Afilias Discovery. Services (ADS), which is free and compatible with EPCglobal standard is based on the opening of the supply chain through the service discovery protocol (ESDS) and ensures interoperability with other systems and supply chain enterprise applications. This protocol could bring a competition of global information services. For more Information see BRIDGE. 2007. "High level design for Discovery Services."

3. IoT Challenges

IoT - sometimes also referred to as the Internet of Everything (IoE) - is ubiquitous intelligence. However and despite its benefits, IoT raises new challenges and amplifies existing ones. Among the main IoT's challenges it should be acknowledged issues related to:

Security. Most IoT devices are not yet capable to process data under a secure manner. This creates a scenario where any wearable devices objects might become a security target. In this sense, security challenges includes measures to prevent data loss, malware, unauthorized access, tracking, monitoring, snooping, skimming, cracking, cloning, sniffing and denial of service. Moreover, this scenario challenges data controllers to keep personal data secure and stresses their obligation to ensure that their subcontractors do likewise. Accordingly, user's lack of control of their own data could effectively develop a form of surveillance that might be unlawful [8]. Also there is a higher risk of users´ lack of control on personal data, particularly when they interact with different type of IoT devices.

Privacy. Even if not all uses of sensors and tags imply privacy concerns, those IoT networks which collect or process information related to identified or identifiable individuals may be subject to privacy risks [9]. Yet along with IoT conveniences and its positives effects, IoT devices might allow retailers and thirds parties to profile consumers' choices and have access to information related to their health, lifestyle, buying habits, and location. Moreover, they might also be able to track their movements without the individual knowledge or prior consent [10]. Finally, another challenge refers to the ability to cross match data and use it for totally different purposes that were not anticipated to the user.

Big data. The analysis, extraction, transformation, storage and processing of high amounts of data may create legal problems such as profiling, behavior analysis and monitoring [11]. Large volumes of data may require coordinated data protection policies, transnational coordination and infrastructure management, among others.

As yet, these challenges have not been addressed by policy makers. However, they reflect a necessity to seek governance solutions to both capitalize IoT strengths and deploy policies to minimize its risks. This leads us to reflect on the hands of who and how this IoT governance should rely.

Accessed 10 November,2015 at http: //www.bridgeproject.eu/data/File/BRIDGEWP02High leveldesignDiscoveryServices. Pdf.
[6] GS1 France is a ONS' service under the administration of Orange Business Services.

4. IoT GOVERNANCE

The IoT Governance can be defined as that area of internet governance that seeks to generate mechanisms and rules to govern devices, infrastructure and functions related to the internet of things [12]. These mechanisms might include a set of actions that are carried out by a multiplicity of actors or stakeholders, namely civil society, governments, academia, private and technical sector that work jointly to identify problems, define solutions and generate arrangements for the implementation, monitoring and evaluation of IoT policies [13]. These stakeholders have, at present, still few meetings[7] to discuss IoT Governance agenda but with a significantly participation of the technical sector. Accordingly, this sector is represented by organizations such as the World Wide Web Consortium (W3C), the Internet Architecture Board (IAB), the Internet Corporation for Assigned Names and Numbers (ICANN), the Internet Research Task Force (IRTF) and the *Internet Engineering Task Force* (IETF) which, jointly with and private actors, are involved in the development of applications and standards for the governance of IoT. In this sense, it appears that only the technical aspects of the IoT network are a priority for IoT Governance at the moment[8]. For this reason and since IoT Governance currently focuses primarily on the infrastructure, applications and standards, I will present the various potential governance models and stakeholders that could possibly participate in IoT Governance in the future.

5. IoT GOVERNANCE AND PUBLIC POLICY IN THE MANAGEMENT OF NETWORK RESOURCES

As stated in (4) it appears that IoT Governance is focused on technical and infrastructural issues and it is carried out mostly by the technical sector. In this vein the question arises: what is the most appropriate model to govern the technical aspects of the current IoT? The answer to this question is not unequivocal and in this sense different positions arise:

---

[7] For example the Dynamic Coalition of the Internet of Things, Internet Governance Forum or the Internet Engineering Task Force.

[8] However it should be point out that this scenario does not imply that such governance should become only technical or only carried out by a technical perspective.

a. *The multistakeholder Internet Governance model should apply to IoT Governance.* This position argues that the governance of IoT can be divided into technical, political and legal issues, where technical aspects of IoT should be addressed by the technical sector while other aspect of IoT Governance should be addressed by other stakeholders as has been done in traditional Internet Governance. This position argues that technical components of IoT Governance agenda should follow the example of the DNS's prior management and be conducted by organizations such as those mentioned in (4) as well as members of the private sector, when appropriate, since these actors often have an adequate means to provide quick and consistent answers necessary for an open, interoperable changing ecosystem.

b. *A new global management agency for technical governance of IoT issues should be created, different from those who have been administering DNS data.* This regulatory position argues that it is possible to create from scratch a new form of regulation of the internet - with an IoT focus - in order to repair certain weaknesses experienced with the DNS management. The argument suggests that it is not possible to include in this management the traditional organizations that have been working on Internet Governance due to the different heterogeneous technologies that IoT embraces, requiring even more specific and complex solutions [14]. Accordingly this line of thought highlights the importance of the technical regulation of IoT since its inception, unlike what happened with the technical regulation of the DNS at the time of emergence of the Internet where different rules where established for the administration of domain names and a singular space was given to the private sector [15, 16]. This governance model could follow either a multistakehoder approach - but with new actors - or suggest a form of multilateral regulation where governments would have a great deal of influence in deciding how IoT Governance would be carried out.

c. *Grant full powers to States in the governance of the resources of IoT infrastructure,* where international organizations such as the International Telecommunications Union would be the logical scope for governments to decide jointly on the governance of a global resource.

Beyond the above mentioned positions, it is possible to think of a new model of IoT Governance where a multistakeholder approach may be implemented but where governments would also have great deal of influence in how IoT Goverance would be achieved. In this sense I argue that a fourth position could contend that IoT Governance should take the form of public-private cooperation for technical solutions to decide the best actions for technical decisions.

6. IoT GOVERNANCE AND THE PUBLIC-PRIVATE COOPERATION FOR TECHNICAL SOLUTIONS

As pointed out in (5), arguments A and C consider IoT Governance as simply a just a new issue that falls under broader Internet Governance - either from a multilateral or multistakeholder approach - while argument B opts for a new environment altogether where regulation is needed due to the specificity of IoT network architecture. The difference between these two kinds of models is not minor, since the role of governments under such regulation is significant given their responsibility to monitor public policies. In this sense, it is helpful to remember that state governments are tools for determining and enforcing public policies to ensure the collective interest and, from my point of view, this traditional conception implies some sort of central role in IoT Governance [17]. But exactly what role do they play?

In order to answer that question, it should firstly be noted that the role of governments in the current IoT Governance debate with regard to the technical aspect of the network is not as active as the role of the technical sector. Indeed it seems that governments themselves prefer to participate in debates related to other issues of Internet Governance rather than those which address the more technical issues related to IoT Governance [18]. This passive role may obey to some kind of naturalization of the management of computing resources by the technical and private sector either by degrees of knowledge or resources-owned. Thereby, the strictly technical issues related to the management of data has not been of significant interest to most governments. It seems that states actors do not want to be involved in the discussion of the technical aspects of IoT Governance which, paradoxically, are the center of the challenges described in (3). It is for this reason that I do argue that states should take action such aspects in the form of a public-private cooperation for technical solutions.

I do define public-private cooperation for technical solutions as the relationship between the public sector and the technical sector - this last could be a private enterprise or an organization such as IETF, W3C among others - where governments implement and monitor actions related to IoT protocols, network standards and infrastructure management. Accordingly, a public–private partnerships with a technical focus have the potential to expand and enhance the effectiveness of government's technical activities related to IoT without diminishing the role of the public sector in the design of public policies.

In this sense, I do believe that governments should take action in the design, management and monitoring of IoT network architecture which, as an integral part of the governance of IoT, should not be considered only as a mere technical aspects unrelated the law and the citizens' rights that depend on it. In this context, states might adopt a new role, specifically focused on supporting transparency and building trust, enabling a permanent dialogue with the technical and private sector and creating creative practices to reflect on and understand the connection between citizens and the corporate world.

If we think technically and politically then participation in the technical-policy making should be part of other public policies conducted by any state. If a technology specification generates a significant political consequence, and if this is the case of IoT, then IoT Governance should include government participation in the technical layer. This intervention would recognize that any influence in protocol design is a political decision just as much as it is a technical one.

Indeed, if a technology specification generates a political consequence, the nature of the processes that result in formulation become relevant to the democratic values of a particular society [19]. The clearest example is privacy by design which is recognized as a field of technical-political decisions [20], combining the expertise of the technical sector with the political action of the government. Relationships in such an environment offer opportunities for shared responsibilities among actors that have both common and divergent interests. Neither stronger government regulation nor technical self-regulation alone will deliver the solutions. Co-regulation combined with transparent bottom-up policy development procedures, can produce frameworks that efficiently combine stability and flexibility for all interested parties but with a public focus. Since Internet protocols are the political governance of the network [21], protocols and technical aspects of IoT should be viewed as a kind of policy-making through IoT Governance, because the impact of these design aspects on the technical architecture inherently represents the exercise of power.

CONCLUSION

Important aspects of IoT need to be further studied and developed in the coming years in regards to its governance. Without a standardized technical approach, it is likely that there will be a proliferation of architectures, identification schemes, protocols and frequencies dedicated to particular and separate uses. This will inevitably lead to a fragmentation of IoT which could hamper its popularity and become a major obstacle in its roll out. Interoperability is a necessity, and inter-tag and inter-sensor communications is a pre-condition for the adoption of IoT to be wide-spread. Furthermore, security measures and privacy concerns are not yet addressed as a priority for governance. Who should decide this governance? How should IoT be governed and how should its governance differ from that of today's Internet? It remains an open question as to whether it should be governed by a state-led agency, a group under the supervision of the United Nations, or an industrial consortium. However, it should be stated that a call for co-regulatory systems involving the technical and the public sector ought to combine the positive values of stable governmental regulation, within and among nation-states, with the flexibility needed to meet the new challenges of globalization in the information age. We live in a transitional period where the old governance system, rooted in the concept of the sovereign nation-state, is increasingly complemented by an emerging new system of governance where all parties should convene and work together towards a solution to avoid that a de-facto standard will eventually appear as in these cases the winning solution is often neither the technically most advanced nor the most socially acceptable one. Currently, the rules applicable to IoT are produced by a number of agencies where states have little or no interference. Most IoT standards to date have been created by agencies in the engineering industry, with relatively small public sector and civil society representation. Public-private partnership for technical cooperation are intended to assist those responsible in complying with data protection legislation and, consequently, to help this technology develop with a sense of respect for fundamental rights. Above all, it should develop a range of different working methods, some yet to be designed. Governments have an obligation to play their part in IoT Governance. There is a new emerging space for dialogue and interaction. A new approach, capable of delivering concrete results for all parties, must be introduced in which governments fill the unique role of facilitating more comprehensive dialogue with the technical sector on IoT issues.

REFERENCES

[1]   Santucci, Gerald. 2012. "RFID and the Internet of Things" Speech presented at the IPV6 Council. Accessed August 24, 2015. http://www.ipv6council.lu/docs/G_Santucci_paper.pdf, last visit August 24 2015.

[2]   Information Society Technology Advisory Group. 1999. *Orientations for Workprogramme 2000 and beyond.* European Union. Accessed August 24, 2015 ftp://ftp.cordis.europa.eu/pub/ist/docs/istag-99-final.pdf.

[3]   Aspis, Analía. 2014, "Internet de las cosas y RFID. ¿políticas públicas o auto-regulación de privados? Un análisis a la luz de la participación de los gobiernos en Net mundial." ("Internet of Things and RFID. Do you publish policies or private self-regulation? An analysis in the light of government involvement in World Net.") Paper presented at the Argentinean Symposium on Computer, San Luis, Argentina, November 13-14.

[4]   Jamoussi, Bilel. 2010. "IoT prospects of worlwide development and current global circumstances." Accessed 19 November, 2015, http://www.itu.int/en/ITU-T/techwatch/Documents/1010-B_Jamoussi_IoT.pdf.

[5]   Recommendation ITU-T Y.2060. 2012. "Overview of the Internet of things." Accessed 18 November, 2015 at http://handle.itu.int/11.1002/1000/11559.

[6]   Jayavardhana, Gubbi and Rajkumar Buyyab. 2013. "Internet of Things (IoT): a vision, architectural elements and future directions," *Future Generation Computer Systems Journal,* 29: 1645–1660.

[7]   Weber, R. 2009. "Internet of things – Need for a new legal environment?" *Computer Law and Security Report,* 25: 522-527.

[8]   Albrecht, Katherine. 2002. Supermarket Cards: The Tip of the Retail Surveillance Iceberg, *Denver University Law Review,* 79: 4.

[9]   Borking, John and Raab, Charles. 2001. "Laws, PETs and Other Technologies for Privacy Protection" Accessed November 19th, 2015 at https://www2.warwick.ac.uk/fac/soc/law/elj/jilt/2001_1/borking/.

[10]   Bennett, Colin and Grant, Rebecca. 2000. Visions of Privacy: Policy Choices for the Digital Age, *Ethics and Information Technology Journal,* 2: 139-144. Accessed 19 November, 2015 at http://link.springer.com/article/10.1023%2FA%3A1010033705593 doi 10.1023/A:1010033705593.

[11] Hunter, Richard. 2002. *World without secrets: business, crime, and privacy in the age of ubiquitous computing.* New York: Wiley.

[12] Unger, Juan León. 2014. "Los gobiernos en la gobernanza de internet: el caso de NetMundial." ("Governments in Internet governance: The case of NetMundial.") Paper presented at the IV Conference of Young Researchers in Law and Social Sciences, University of Buenos Aires, Buenos Aires, Argentina, September 17-19.

[13] Banks, Karen. 2005. "Summitry and strategies," *Index on Censorship*, Vol 3: 85-91, doi 10.1080/03064220500258992, accessed 10 November, 2015 at http://www.tandfonline.com/doi/abs/10.1080/03064220500 258992?journalCode=rioc20.

[14] Internet of Things European Research Cluster. 2015. "The Internet of Things. IoT Governance, Privacy and Security Issues." Accessed November, 15, 2015 at www.internet-of-thingsresearch.eu/pdf/IERC_ Position_Paper_IoT_Governance_Privacy_Security_Final.pdf.

[15] National Telecommunications and Information Administration. 1998. "Management of Internet Names and Addresses." Accessed 10 November, 2015 at https://www.icann.org/resources/unthemed-pages/white-paper-2 012-02-25-en.

[16] Kleinwachter, Wolfgang. 2003. "From Self-Governance to Public-Private Partnership: The Changing Role of Governments in the Management of the Internet's Core Resources" *Loyola of Los Angeles Law Review,* 36:1103.

[17] Aspis, Analía. 2014. "Tecnología, sociedad latinoamericana y gobernanza de internet." ("Technology, Latin American society and internet governance.") Paper presented at the Second Conference of the Institute for the Study of Latin America and the Caribbean, University of Buenos Aires, Buenos Aires, September 24-26.

[18] DeNardis, Laura. (2009). *Protocol Politics: The Globalization of Internet Governance.* Cambridge: MIT Press.

[19] Fischer-Hübner, Simone. 2001. *IT-security and privacy: design and use of privacy-enhancing security mechanisms.* New York: Springer.

[20] DeNardis, Laura (2014). *The Global War for Internet Governance.* London: Yale University Press.

BIOGRAPHICAL SKETCH

Name: Analia Aspis
Affiliation: University oOf Buenos Aires
Date of Birth: 8-3-1980
Education: Lawyer (MBA). PhD candidate
Address: Medrano 1670 – 13 A

The author is lawyer graduated with honors at the University of Buenos Aires. She has a Master in Law Legal Issues, Crime and Security of New Technologies at the University of Lausanne (Switzerland) and a PhD candidate at the University of Buenos Aires on the subject Consumers privacy and Internet of Things. She has been invited professor of Law and Informatics in Colombia, Peru, Mexico and Sweden. She has been researcher at the Swedish Law and Informatics Research Institute at University of Stockholm (Sweden) as well as researcher and coordinator of the Research Project on Surveillance and Human Rights and the Interdisciplinary Study Group on Internet Governance. With regard her professional experience, Ms. Aspis is an independent IT consultant at Wayna consultants, policy advisor on open government and transparency policies (Mexico), president of the Argentina Hub for Internet Governance, Internet Governance Caucus co-coordinator, founder and president of Weiba Foundation.

Research and Professional Experience:

Doctoral Researcher (Conicet) in law and new technologies, Ambrosio Gioja Law Research Institute, Faculty of Law and Social Sciences, University of Buenos Aires. Subject: Consumers

Master of Law (MLaw) in Legal Issues, Crime and Security of New Technologies, University of Lausanne, Switzerland. Master these subject: Comparative study between US, EU and Swiss consumer law protection and RFID.

Lawyer. Law Degree. Honour Diploma, Faculty of Law and Social Sciences University of Buenos Aires. Average 9/10. Specialization: Commercial, Consumer and Corporate Law and International Law.

External Professor and Researcher on Transparency, Open Government and Accountability in the Autonomous University of Baja California, School of Economics and International Relations, México.

Professor and Coordinator of the interdisciplinary study group on Internet governance, University of Buenos Aires.

Researcher and Coordinator of the research project on Surveillance and Human Rights -UBACyT and DECyT, University of Buenos Aires.

Academia's representative at the Working Group for an Internet Free and Secure. (2014-2016)

Visiting Professor, Privacy and RFID, Faculty of Communication, Colombian Polytechnic University, Bogotá, Colombia.

IT Law Invited Professor, Catholic University of Lima, Peru.

Specialization in Computer Crimes and Computer Evidence, Professional Training Program, Lawyers Bar of Buenos Aires, Argentina.

Researcher, The Swedish Law and Informatics Research Institute, Faculty of Law, University of Stockholm, Sweden. Subject: RFID and consumer privacy rights

Senior Lecturer of the Master Programme in Law and Information Technology, Faculty of Law, University of Stockholm, Sweden

Professional Appointments:

Independent ICT Consultant

Member of the Stakeholder Selection Committee for the PGA Consultation on WSIS+10 (2 July 2015) and the High-level Meeting December 2015

Collaborator at the NCUC Meeting at Buenos Aires, 2015.

Global Internet Governance Academic Network, Member of the Committee for Selection of new members and speakers at the IGF Forum.

Founder and President of Weiba Foundation, Buenos Aires, Argentina.

IGF Hub Forum National Organizer, United Nations, Buenos Aires, Argentina

Policy Advisor on Open Government and Transparency Policies, Mexican Parliament.

Internet Governance Caucus Co-coordinator

Academic Committee Member of the E-Marc Congress on Online dispute resolution

Argentina Hub Internet Governance President

Internet Governance Forum Argentinean Hub responsible

Representative of Argentina at the United Nations Conference on Trade and Development (UNCTAD)

Argentinian Hub Coordinator for the WSIS + 10 NETMundial, Eurodig and ICANN meeting.

Data Protection Specialist, Generis Company Builders, Argentina.

Editor Writer At Caselex. ICT and Media Law, Amsterdam, Netherlands

Researcher and Lecturer at the Institute of Law and New Technology, Stockholm, Sweden

Researcher on International Law. Subject: Law norms superposition and regional blocks: its relation with the World Trade Organization, Centre of Industrial and Economic Rights, University of Buenos Aires.

Publications Last 3 Years:

–   The Involvement of Governments in the Governance of the Internet of Things and the Management of Resources: the Political Element in the Technical Design of the Network, Connaiisi, UTN University, Argentina.
–   The Singular Political Multistakeholder Model, Gino Germani Institute, Argentina.
–   Remote Participation and Internet Governance: Challenges of the Digital Citizenship, Jaiio, Argentina.
–   Internet of Things and RFID: Public Policies or Private Self regulation? An Analysis in the Light of Net Mundial Government Participation. Argentina.
–   Technology, Latin American Society and Internet Governance, II Jornadas del Instituto de Estudios de América Latina y el Caribe (Second Conference of the Institute for the Study of Latin America and the Caribbean.)
–   Technology, Society and Internet Governance, Ishir-Conicet y Centro de Estudios Culturales (Ishir-Conicet and Cultural Studies Center), Rosario, Argentina.
–   Access Public Information and Business Improvement, Ecuador. (co-author).
–   The Model of Open Government in Latin America. the Dilemma of the Structures and the Phenomenon of Corruption. Spain (co-author).
–   Blogging and E-Democracy, Revista Pensar en Derecho, Facultad de Derecho, Universidad de Buenos Aires (Think Magazine Law, Faculty of Law, University of Buenos Aires).

- RFID and Internet of Things, Cutter IT Journal, Arlington, Estados Unidos.
- RFID and Cybercrime, Iberoamerican Federation of IT Law Summit, Santa Cruz, Bolivia. Memories of the Congress.
- The Impact of Technology and the Law, (in process), Ed. Ad-hoc, Buenos Aires, Argentina.
- ICT as an Alternative Judiciary Paradigm (editorial process), Ed. Errepar, Buenos Aires, Argentina.
- ICT and the Role of Justice in Latinoamerica, Law and Society Journal, November 2010, Lima, Perú.
- E-Luxe, Echos Money magazine, Junior Enterprise, High Commercial School (HEC), University of Lausanne, n° 13 2007, p.45, Lausanne, Switzerland.
- Contractual Aspect of E-Commerce Errepar, Buenos Aires, Argentina.

BIBLIOGRAPHY

2014 IEEE World Forum on Internet of Things (WF-IoT 2014): Seoul, South Korea, 6-8 March 2014. LCCN: 2015301025 Main title: 2014 IEEE World Forum on Internet of Things (WF-IoT 2014): Seoul, South Korea, 6-8 March 2014. Published/Produced: Piscataway, NJ: IEEE; Red Hook, NY: Curan Associates, Inc. [distributor], [2014] Description: 580 pages: illustrations; 27 cm ISBN: 9781479950713 (pbk.) Notes: "IEEE Catalog Number: CFP1418V-POD." Includes bibliographical references and index.

2014 International Conference on the Internet of Things (IOT 2014): Cambridge, Massachusetts, USA 6-8 October 2014. LCCN: 2015472880 Meeting name: IOT (Conference) (2014: Cambridge, Mass.) Main title: 2014 International Conference on the Internet of Things (IOT 2014): Cambridge, Massachusetts, USA 6-8 October 2014. Published/Produced: Piscataway, NJ: IEEE, [2014] Description: 107 pages: illustrations; 28 cm ISBN: 9781479951550 LC classification: QA76.5915.I72 2014 Subjects: Ubiquitous computing--Congresses. Embedded Internet devices--Congresses. Wireless communication systems--Congresses. Ambient intelligence--Congresses. Interactive computer systems--Congresses. Sensor networks--Congresses. Radio frequency identification systems--Congresses. Internet--Congresses. Notes: "IEEE Catalog Number: CFP1414K-

POD." Includes bibliographical references.

Advanced technological solutions for e-Health and dementia patient monitoring LCCN: 2014045013 Main title: Advanced technological solutions for e-Health and dementia patient monitoring / Fatos Xhafa, Universitat Politècnica de Catalunya, Spain; Philip Moore, School of Information Science and Engineering, Lanzhou University, China; George Tadros, University of Warwick, UK. Published/Produced: Hershey, PA: Medical Information Science Reference, [2015] Description: xxvi, 389 pages: illustrations; 29 cm. ISBN: 9781466674813 (hardcover) LC classification: RC521.A29 2015 Related names: Xhafa, Fatos, editor. Moore, Philip, 1947- editor. Tadros, George, 1962- editor. Summary: "This book provides comprehensive coverage of issues in patient health and support from the perspectives of doctors, nurses, patients, and caregivers with a focus on challenges and opportunities, as well as future research in the field"--Provided by publisher. Contents: Behavioural and psychological symptoms in dementia / Nikhila Deshpande, Babu Naya -- Carers of people with dementia and the use of assistive technologies / Sarmishtha Bhattacharyya, Susan Mary Benbow -- Intelligently adaptive mobile interfaces for older people / Sheila Mc Carthy, Heather Sayers, Paul Mc Kevitt, Mike McTear, Kieran Coyle -- Emerging technologies for dementia patient monitoring / Tarik Qassem -- Employing opportunistic networks in dementia patient monitoring / Radu-Ioan Ciobanu, Ciprian Dobre -- An autonomous intelligent system for the private outdoors monitoring of people with mild cognitive impairments / Antoni Martínez-Ballesté, Frederic Borràs, Agusti Solanas -- Service evolution in clouds for dementia patient monitoring system usability enhancement / Zhe Wang, Chalmers Kevin, Xiaodong Liu, Guojian Cheng -- NoSQL technologies for real time (patient) monitoring / Ciprian Dobre, Fatos Xhafa -- Cloud based monitoring for patients with dementia / Philip Moore, Fatos Xhafa, Mak Sharma -- Fostering independent living in the aging population through proactive paging / Mauro Migliardi, Cristiana Degano, Marco Tettamanti -- Using smart phone as a track and fall detector: an intelligent support system for people with dementia / Chia-Yin Ko, Fang-Yie Leu, I-Tsen -- Pervasive data capturing and analysis for patients with Alzheimer's disease / Kam-Yiu Lam [and 5 more] -- An internet of things governance architecture with applications in healthcare / Adrian Copie, Bogdan Manae, Victor Ion Munteanu, Teodor-Florin Fortie. Subjects: Dementia--Patients--Care. Wireless communication systems in medical care. Patient monitoring--Equipment and supplies. Telecommunication in medicine--Methods. Dementia. Monitoring, Physiologic--instrumentation. Monitoring, Physiologic--methods. Self-Help Devices. Telemedicine--instrumentation. Telemedicine--methods. Notes: Includes bibliographical references (pages 345-379) and index. Series: Advances in medical, technological, and clinical practice book (AMTCP) book series, 2327-9354 Premier reference source

Advances onto the Internet of Things: how ontologies make the Internet of Things meaningful LCCN: 2013957383 Main title: Advances onto the Internet of Things: how

ontologies make the Internet of Things meaningful / Salvatore Gaglio, Giuseppe Lo Re, editors. Published/Produced: Cham; New York: Springer-Verlag, [2014] ©2014 Description: ix, 352 pages: illustrations, 24 cm. Links: Publisher description http://www.loc.gov/catdir/enhancements/fy1405/2013957383-d.html Table of contents only http://www.loc.gov/catdir/enhancements/fy1405/2013957383-t.html ISBN: 9783319039916 3319039911 LC classification: TK7895.E43 A39 2014 Related names: Gaglio, S. (Salvatore), 1954- editor. Lo Re, Giuseppe, editor Summary: The title of this book is a pun on the use of the preposition onto with the aim of recalling "Ontology", the term commonly adopted in the computer science community to indicate the study of the formal specification for organizing knowledge. In the field of knowledge engineering, Ontologies are used for modeling concepts and relationships on some domain. The year 2013 celebrates the twentieth anniversary of the World Wide Web. The simple network of hypermedia has transformed the world of communications with enormous implications on the social relationships. However, traditional World Wide Web is currently experiencing a challenging evolution toward the Internet of Things (IoT), today feasible thanks to the integration of pervasive technologies capable of sensing the environment. The most important contribution of IoT regards the possibility of enabling more efficient machine-to-machine cooperation. To such aim, ontologies represent the most suitable tool to enable transfer and comprehension of information among computer applications, even those designed and developed by unrelated people in different places. This book proposes a collection of contributions illustrating different applications following these directions and that are the outcomes of real experiences developed in the context of research projects.-- Source other than Library of Congress. Subjects: Internet of things. Embedded Internet devices. Notes: Includes bibliographical references. Series: Advances in intelligent systems and computing; 260 Advances in intelligent systems and computing; 260.

Big data and internet of things: a roadmap for smart environments

LCCN: 2014934460 Main title: Big data and internet of things: a roadmap for smart environments / Nik Bessis, Ciprian Dobre, editors. Published/Produced: Cham: Springer, [2014] ©2014 Description: xix, 470 pages: illustrations; 25 cm. ISBN: 9783319050287 3319050281 LC classification: QA76.9.B45 B55 2014 Related names: Bessis, Nik, 1967- editor. Dobre, Ciprian, editor. Contents: Machine generated contents note: pt. I Foundations and Principles -- Big Data Platforms for the Internet of Things / Florin Pop -- Improving Data and Service Interoperability with Structure, Compliance, Conformance and Context Awareness / Jose C. Delgado -- Big Data Management Systems for the Exploitation of Pervasive Environments / Salvalore Venticinque -- On RFID False Authentications / Congfu Xu -- Adaptive Pipelined Neural Network Structure in Self-aware Internet of Things / Ciprian Dobre -- Spatial Dimensions of Big Data: Application of Geographical Concepts and Spatial Technology to the Internet of Things / Henk Scholten -- Fog Computing: A Platform for Internet of Things and Analytics / Jiang Zhu -- pt. II Advanced Models and

Architectures -- Big Data Metadata Management in Smart Grids / Andreas Prinz -- Context-Aware Dynamic Discovery and Configuration of 'Things' in Smart Environments / Dimitrios Georgakopoulos -- Contents note continued: Simultaneous Analysis of Multiple Big Data Networks: Mapping Graphs into a Data Model / Mohamed Dbouk -- Toward Web Enhanced Building Automation Systems / Jean Hennebert -- Intelligent Transportation Systems and Wireless Access in Vehicular Environment Technology for Developing Smart Cities / Nik Bessis -- Emerging Technologies in Health Information Systems: Genomics Driven Wellness Tracking and Management System (GO-WELL) / Yesim Aydin Son -- pt. III Advanced Applications and Future Trends -- Sustainability Data and Analytics in Cloud-Based M2M Systems / Schahram Dustdar -- Social Networking Analysis / Niamh Curran -- Leveraging Social Media and IoT to Bootstrap Smart Environments / John G. Breslin -- Four-Layer Architecture for Product Traceability in Logistic Applications / Jose Manuel Pastor -- Disaster Evacuation Guidance Using Opportunistic Communication: The Potential for Opportunity-Based Service / Hiroyoshi Miwa. Subjects: Big data. Internet of things. Context-aware computing. Big data. Context-aware computing. Internet of things. Notes: Includes bibliographical references. Series: Studies in Computational Intelligence, 1860-949X; volume 546 Studies in computational intelligence; v.546. 1860-949X

Big Data and the Internet of Things: enterprise information architecture for a new age LCCN: 2015487628 Personal name: Stackowiak, Robert, author. Main title: Big Data and the Internet of Things: enterprise information architecture for a new age / Robert Stackowiak, Art Licht, Venu Mantha, Louis Nagode. Published/Produced: [New York]: Apress, [2015] New York: Springer Science+Business Media New York ©2015 Description: xviii, 197 pages: illustrations; 23 cm. ISBN: 1484209877 9781484209875 LC classification: QA76.9.D343 S6843 2015 Portion of title: Enterprise information architecture for a new age Related names: Licht, Art, author. Mantha, Venu, author.

Nagode, Louis, author.
Summary: "Your guide to defining an information architecture for emerging trends like Big Data and the Internet of Things"--Page 1 of cover. Contents: Big Data solutions and the Internet of Things -- Evaluating the art of the possible -- Understanding the business -- Business information mapping for Big Data and the Internet of Things -- Understanding organizational skills -- Designing the future state information architecture -- Defining an initial plan and roadmap -- Implementing the plan. Subjects: Big data. Internet of things. Management information systems. Notes: Includes bibliographical references (pages 181-183) and index.

Challenges, opportunities, and dimensions of cyber-physical systems LCCN: 2014036866 Personal name: Krishna, P. Venkata, 1977- Main title: Challenges, opportunities, and dimensions of cyber-physical systems / P. Venkata Krishna, V. Saritha, H.P. Sultana. Published/Produced: Hershey, PA: Information Science Reference, an imprint of IGI Global, [2015] Description: xiv, 314 pages: illustrations; 29 cm.

ISBN: 9781466673120 (hardcover) 9781466673151 (print and perpetual access) LC classification: TK7895.E43 K75 2015 Related names: Saritha, V., 1977- Sultana, H. P., 1973- Summary: "This book explores current trends and enhancements of CPS, highlighting the critical need for further research and advancement in this field and focusing on architectural fundamentals, interdisciplinary functions, and futuristic implications"-- Provided by publisher. Subjects: Embedded computer systems. Embedded Internet devices. Internet of things. Ad hoc networks (Computer networks) Notes: Includes bibliographical references (pages 306-311) and index. Series: A volume in the advances in systems analysis, software engineering, and high performance computing (ASASEHPC) book series

China's geoinformation industry 2015 LCCN: 2015042272 Uniform title: Ce hui di li xin xi zhuan xing sheng ji yan jiu bao gao. English. Main title: China's geoinformation industry 2015 / volume editor, Kurexi Maihesuti, National Administration of Surveying, Mapping and Geoinformation, Beijing, CHINA. Edition: First

Edition. Published/Produced: Minneapolis, MN: East View Press, 2015. Description: pages cm. ISBN: 9781879944671 (pbk.) 1879944677 (pbk.) LC classification: G70.215.C6 C413 2015 Related names: Kurexi, Maihesuti, 1960- editor of compilation. Contents: Ongoing reforms in the surveying, mapping and geoinformation industry / Kurexi Maihesuti -- China's national priorities in the surveying, mapping and geoinformation industry / Xu Yongqing, Qiao Chaofei, Liu Li, Ruan Yuzhou and Ning Zhenya -- Geoinformation in the Chinese capital: new developments at the Beijing Institute of Surveying and Mapping / Wen Zongyong -- View from a coastal province: Zhejiang's surveying, mapping and geoinformation industry / Chen Jianguo -- China's newest mega-city: Chongqing's transformation of the surveying, mapping and geoinformation industry / Zhang Yuan -- China's deep south: Sichuan Province's development of the surveying, mapping and geoinformation industry / Ma Yun -- China's surveying, mapping and geoinformation sector: law and legal reform issues / Wang Baoli -- Taking country-wide geospatial sector reforms to key provinces: the Jiangxi experience / Gao Zhenhua -- China's national leadership directives for the surveying, mapping and geoinformation industry: challenges and transformation / Liu Li -- China's national geographic census / Li Weisen -- Mineral resources: interplay of remote sensing and on-site monitoring / Lu Xiaoping, Cheng Gang and Ge Xiaosan -- Anticipating user demand for China's national geographic census / Wang Hua, Chen Xiaoqian and Zhang Kai. China's map publishing industry: Sinomaps in 2015 and beyond / Zhao Xiaoming -- Satellite navigation and location-based services: China's Beidou GNSS and more / Miao Qianjun -- China's geoinformation industry: themes for 2015 / Cao Tianjing, Sun Xiaopeng, Liang Peng and Rong Wei -- China and the global internet: geospatial private sector embraces "mobile internet" and "internet of things" / Wang Kanghong -- Traditional and state-owned geoinformation enterprises: new challenges ahead / Yang Zhenpeng -- Learning from mistakes: applying "internet thinking" to China's geoinformation industry / Xu Yong -- A view from China's military: innovation in the geoinformation industry /

Wang Jiayao and Cui Xiaojie --
The transformation of Autonavi
in the mobile internet and big
data era / Dong Zhenning, Wang
Yujing, Chen Shuiping and
Zhou Qi -- China's virtual
reality: the live 3-d image map
industry in the big data era /
Wan Heping, Yuan Jianfeng,
Ding Yong and Li Yuqi --
China's first high-security
geospatial database management
system: beyonDB and protecting
national geoinformation assets /
Guo Xinping, Shang Dong,
Chen Rongguo and Xie Jiong.
Subjects: Geographic
information systems--China.
Geodatabases--China. Series:
East View special intelligence
reports

Collaborative internet of things (C-
IoT): for future smart connected
life and business LCCN:
2015008308 Personal name:
Behmann, Fawzi. Main title:
Collaborative internet of things
(C-IoT): for future smart
connected life and business /
Fawzi Behmann, Kwok Wu.
Published/Produced: Hoboken:
John Wiley and Sons, Inc., 2015.
Description: pages cm Links:
Cover image
http://catalogimages.wiley.com/i
mages/db/jimages/97811189137
41.jpg ISBN: 9781118913741
(hardback) LC classification:
TK7895.E43 B44 2015 Related
names: Wu, Kwok. Summary:
"Provides a simplified visionary
approach about the future
direction of IoT, addressing its
wide-scale adoption in many
markets, its interception with
advanced technology, the
explosive growth in data, and
the emergence of data
analytics"-- Provided by
publisher. Contents: Machine
generated contents note:
Contents Forward Preface 1.
INTRODUCTIONS AND
MOTIVATION 1.1 Introduction
1.2 The book 1.2.1 Objectives
1.2.2 Benefits 1.2.3
Organization 1.2.4 Book Cover
1.2.5 Impact of C-IoT 1.2.6
Summary 1.3 C-IoT Terms of
References 1.3.1 Introduction
1.3.2 Need for IoT Framework
1.3.3 C-IoT Domains and
Business Apps Model 1.3.4 C-
IoT Roadmap 1.3.5 C-IoT
Platform and Developer
Community 1.3.6 C-IoT
Opportunities for Business apps,
solutions and systems 1.4 The
Future 1.4.1 General Trends
1.4.2 Point Solutions 1.4.3
Collaborative IoT 1.4.4 C-IoT
and RFID 1.4.5 C-IoT and
Nanotechnology 1.4.6 Cyber-
Collaborative IoT (C2-IoT) 1.4.7
C2-IoT and EBOLA Case 1.4.8
Summary 2. APPLICATION
REQUIREMENTS 2.1 C-IOT

Landscape 2.1.1 C-IoT Model and Architecture Layers 2.1.2 C-IoT Model and Enabling Technologies 2.1.3 Definition of key elements 2.1.4 Requirement Considerations 2.1.5 C-IoT System Solution - Requirement Considerations 2.2 Applications Requirement - Use Cases 2.3 Health and Fitness (Lead Example) 2.3.1 Landscape 2.3.2 Health and Fitness - Sensing Requirements 2.3.3 Health and Fitness - Gateway Requirements 2.3.4 Health and Fitness - Service Requirements 2.3.5 Health and Fitness - Solution Considerations 2.3.6 Health and Fitness - System Considerations 2.3.7 Health and Fitness and Hospitals 2.4 Video Surveillance 2.4.1 Landscape 2.4.2 Video Surveillance - Across Home, Industry and Infrastructure 2.4.3 Video Surveillance - Sensing Requirements 2.4.4 Video Surveillance - Gateway Requirements 2.4.5 Video Surveillance - Services 2.4.6 Example: Red Light Camera - Photo Enforcement Camera 2.4.7 Conclusion 2.5 Smart Home and Building 2.5.1 Landscape 2.5.2 Requirement 2.5.3 Home - Sensing Requirements 2.5.4 Home - Gateway Requirements 2.5.5 Home - Services 2.6 Smart Energy 2.6.1 Landscape 2.6.2 Requirements 2.6.3 Smart Energy - Sensing Requirements 2.6.4 Smart Energy - Gateway Requirements 2.6.5 Smart Energy - Services 2.6.6 The Smart Energy App 2.6.7 Smart Energy and Network Security 2.7 Track and Monitor 2.7.1 Landscape 2.7.2 Track and Monitory - Sensing Requirements 2.7.3 Track and Monitor - Services 2.7.4 Track and Monitor - Solution Considerations 2.7.5 Track and Monitor - Examples 2.8 Smart Factory/Manufacturing 2.8.1 Factory Automation - Robot 2.8.2 Caregiver and Robot 2.8.3 Industrial Robot 2.9 Others: Smart Car, Smart Truck and Smart City 2.9.1 Smart Car 2.9.2 Smart Roadside 2.9.3 Drone 2.9.4 Machine Vision 2.9.5 Smart City 3. C-IOT APPLICATIONS AND SERVICES 3.1 Smart IoT Application Use Cases 3.1.1 Health monitoring - Individual level (Fitness/Health Tracking wearables) 3.1.2 Health Monitoring at Business level (used in clinic) 3.1.3 Home and Building Automation - Individual level (Smart Home) 3.1.3.1 Smart Thermostat (Smart Energy Management) 3.1.3.2 Smart Smoke Alarm (Safety) 3.1.3.3 Smart IP Camera for Video Surveillance (Security)

Sustainability 7. CONCLUSION 7.1 Simple C-IoT Domains and Model 7.2 Disruptive Business Applications of C-IoT 7.3 A New LifeStyle 7.4 Development Platform 7.5 C-IoT emerging Standards, Consortiums and other Initiatives 7.5.1 C-IoT Emerging Standards 7.5.2 C-IoT Emerging Consortiums 7.5.3 Forums, Workshops, and other Initiatives 7.5.4 C-IoT and Radio Communications 7.5.5 C-IoT and Nanotechnology 7.5.6 C-IoT and Security 7.6 Final Note References About the Authors Index. Subjects: Embedded Internet devices. Internet of things. Technology and Engineering / Mobile and Wireless Communications. Notes: Includes bibliographical references and index. Additional formats: Online version: Behmann, Fawzi. Collaborative internet of things (C-IoT) Hoboken: John Wiley and Sons, Inc., 2015 9781118913727 (DLC) 2015011725

Communications and competition law: key issues in the telecoms, media and technology sectors LCCN: 2015372356 Main title: Communications and competition law: key issues in the telecoms, media and technology sectors / edited by Fabrizio Cugia di Sant' Orsola, Rehman Noormohamed, Denis Alves Guimarães. Published/Produced: Alphen aan den Rijn, The Netherlands: Kluwer Law International, [2015] Description: lxiii, 423 pages: illustrations; 25 cm. Links: Table of contents only http://www.loc.gov/catdir/toc/fy16pdf02/2015372356.html ISBN: 9789041151469 (hbk.: alk. paper) 904115146X (hbk.: alk. paper) LC classification: K4304.8.C66 2015 Related names: Cugia, Fabrizio, 1963- editor. Noormohamed, Rehman, editor. Alves Guimarães, Denis, editor. International Bar Association, sponsoring body. Contents: Introducing Diversity in EU Merger Control / Yvan Desmedt and Philippe Laconte -- Summary of Recent U.S. Enforcement Decisions in Communication/Entertainment Industry Transactions / Ilene Knable Gotts -- Competition and Regulatory Aspects of Convergence, Takeovers and Mergers in the Communications and Media Industries /Thomas Janssens and Joep Wolfhagen -- Brazil's Antitrust and Regulatory Reviews of TIM/Telefonica: Lessons Learned / Ana Paula Martinez and Alexandre Ditzel Faraco -- Changes in the Global Telecommunication Market and Its Implications in Brazil /

Gesner Oliveira and Wagner Heibel -- Mergers in the Canadian Communications Sector: An Increasingly Curious Situation / Lorne Salzman -- In Search of a Competition Doctrine for Information Technology Markets: Recent Antitrust Developments in the Online Sector / Jeffrey A. Eisenach and Ilene Knable Gotts -- The Internet of Things in the Light of Digitalization and Increased Media Convergence / Anna Blume Huttenlauch and Thoralf Knuth -- Dynamic Markets and Competition Policy / Bernardo Macedo and Sílvia Fagá De Almeida -- Recent Antitrust Developments in the Online Sector / Federico Marini-Balestra -- Mobile Payments and Mobile Banking in Brazil: Perspectives from an Emerging Market / Márcio Issao Nakane, Camila Yumy Saito and Mariana Oliveira e Silva -- Internet of Things: Manufacturing Companies Industry and Use of "White Spectrum": Ghost in the Machine? / Kurt Tiam and Andy Huang -- Competitive Aspects of Cloud-Based Services / Fabrizio Cugia di Sant'Orsola and Silvia Giampaolo -- Standard-Essential Patents and US Antitrust Law: Light at the End of the Tunnel? / Leon B. Greenfield, Hartmut Schneider

and Perry A. Lange -- IP and Antitrust: Recent Developments in EU Law / Miguel Rato and Mark English -- Antitrust Cases Involving Intellectual Property Rights in the Communication and Media Sector in Brazil / Barbara Rosenberg, Luis Bernardo Cascão and Vivian Terng -- Patents Meet Antitrust Law: The State of Play of the FRAND Defense in Germany / Wolrad Prinz zu Waldeck und Pyrmont -- The Role of Privacy in a Changing World / Chris Boam -- The Transatlantic Perspective: Data Protection and Competition Law Pamela Jones Harbour / Power over Data: Brazil in Times of Digital Uncertainty / Floriano De Azevedo Marques Neto, Milene Louise Renée Coscione and Juliana Deguirmendjian -- Big Data and the Cloud: Privacy and Security Threats of Mass Digital Surveillance? / Lyda Mastrantonio and Natalia Porto --Net Neutrality Regulation: A Worldwide Overview and the Chilean Pioneer's Experience / Alfonso Silva and Sebastian Squella -- Net Neutrality in Singapore: A Fair Game / Chung Nian Lam -- Internet Regulation in Brazil: The Network Neutrality Issue / Lauro Celidonio Gomes dos Reis Neto, Fabio Ferreira Kujawski and

Thays Castaldi Gentil -- The New Brazilian Internet Constitution and the Netmundial Forum / João Moura -- The Brazilian Telecom Regulatory Scenario and the Proposals of the Internet Law / Regina Ribeiro do Valle -- Competition in the Brazilian Telecommunication Market / Maximiliano Martinhão, Guido Lorencini Schuina, Haitam Laboissiere Naser and Leonardo Fernandez Zagonn -- A New Horizon for Competition Advocacy in Brazil Adriano Augusto do Couto Costa, Marcelo de Matos Ramos and Roberto Domingos Taufick -- Overlaps and Synergies between Regulators in the Brazilian Telecommunications / Market Marcelo Bechara de Souza Hobaika and Carlos M. Baigorri -- The New Competition Law in Brazil and the New Framework for Merger Analysis in Telecom / Carlos Emmanuel Joppert Ragazzo and Cristiane Landerdahl de Albuquerque -- Regulatory Policy Round Table: A Dialogue between Telecommunications and Antitrust Authorities Denis / Alves Guimarães. Subjects: Telecommunication--Law and legislation--Congresses. Antitrust law--Congresses. Internet--Law and legislation-- Congresses. Telecommunication--Law and legislation--Brazil--Congresses. Antitrust law--Brazil-- Congresses. Internet--Law and legislation--Brazil--Congresses. Notes: Papers and contributions from two gatherings of the Communications and Competition International Bar Association Committees, held in Rio de Janeiro in 2013 and in Prague in 2014. Includes bibliographical references and index. Series: International Bar Association Series 25

Cyber security: an introduction for non-technical managers LCCN: 2015010130 Personal name: Green, Jeremy Swinfen. Main title: Cyber security: an introduction for non-technical managers / Jeremy Swinfen Green, Mosoco Ltd, London, UK. Published/Produced: Farnham, Surrey; Burlington, VT: Gower, [2015] Description: vi, 255 pages; 23 cm ISBN: 9781472466730 (hardback: alk. paper) LC classification: HF5548.37.G737 2015 Contents: Cyber security and cyber risk -- A holistic approach to cyber security -- The scope of cyber security -- Systems risks -- People and networks -- Cloud computing -- Bring your own device -- Protecting people --

Keeping data secure outside the office -- Social media risk -- Who is stealing your organisation's identity? -- Disposing of data safely -- The internet of things -- Developing a cyber security strategy -- Picking the right team -- Getting prepared -- Developing a risk register -- Managing the impact of cyber incidents -- Responding to incidents -- Digital governance -- Afterword: looking from the past to the future. Subjects: Business enterprises--Computer networks--Security measures. Computer security. Corporations--Security measures. Computer crimes--Prevention. Notes: Includes bibliographical references and index.

Cybersecurity in our Digital Lives LCCN: 2014958091 Main title: Cybersecurity in our Digital Lives / edited by Jane LeClair and Gregory Keeley, foreward by John Ashcroft. Published/Produced: Albany, NY: Hudson Whitman, 2015. Description: xvi, 243 pages; 22 cm ISBN: 9780989845144 0989845141 LC classification: QA76.9.A25 C955 2015 Related names: LeClair, Jane, editor. Keeley, Gregory, editor. Ashcroft, John, foreword. Summary: "Did you know your car can be hacked? Your medical device? Your employers HVAC system? Are you aware that bringing your own device to work may have security implications? Consumers of digital technology are often familiar with headline-making hacks and breaches, but lack a complete understanding of how and why they happen, or if they have been professionally or personally compromised. In Cybersecurity in Our Digital Lives, twelve experts provide much-needed clarification on the technology behind our daily digital interactions. They explain such things as supply chain, Internet of Things, social media, cloud computing, mobile devices, the C-Suite, social engineering, and legal confidentially. Then, they discuss very real threats, make suggestions about what can be done to enhance security, and offer recommendations for best practices. An ideal resource for students, practitioners, employers, and anyone who uses digital products and services."-- Publisher Subjects: Cyber intelligence (Computer security) Cyber intelligence (Computer security) Notes: Includes bibliographical references and index. Series: Protecting Our Future Protecting Our Future.

Designing for emerging technologies: UX for Genomics, Robotics, and the Internet of Things LCCN: 2015304740 Main title: Designing for emerging technologies: UX for Genomics, Robotics, and the Internet of Things / edited by Jonathan Follett. Edition: First edition. Published/Produced: Sebastopol, CA: O'Reilly, 2014. ©2015 Description: xxi, 479 pages: illustrations (chiefly color); 23 cm ISBN: 9781449370510 (pbk.) 1449370519 (pbk.) LC classification: QA76.9.U83 D468 2014 Related names: Follett, Jonathan, editor. Summary: "The recent digital and mobile revolutions are a minor blip compared to the next wave of technological change, as everything from robot swarms to skin-top embeddable computers and bio printable organs start appearing in coming years. In this collection of inspiring essays, designers, engineers, and researchers discuss their approaches to experience design for groundbreaking technologies. Design not only provides the framework for how technology works and how it's used, but also places it in a broader context that includes the total ecosystem with which it interacts and the possibility of unintended consequences. If you're a UX designer or engineer open to complexity and dissonant ideas, this book is a revelation"--Back cover. Contents: Designing for emerging technologies / Jonathan Follett -- Intelligent materials: designing material behavior / Brook Kennedy -- Taking control of gesture interaction / Gershom Kutliroff, Yaron Yanai -- Fashion with function: designing for wearables / Michal Levin -- Learning ang thinking with things / Stephen P. Anderson -- Designing for collaborative robotics / Jeff Faneuff -- Design takes on new dimensions: evolving visualization approaches for neuroscience and cosmology / Hunter Whitney -- Embeddables: the next evolution of wearable tech / Andy Goodman -- Prototyping interactive objects / Scott Sullivan -- Emerging technology and toy design / Barry Kudrowitz -- Musical instrument design / Camille Goudeseune -- Design for life / Juhan Sonin -- Architecture as interface: advocating a hybrid design approach for interconnected environments / Erin Rae Hoffer -- Design for the networked world: a practice for the twenty-first century / Matt Nish-Lapidus

-- New responsibilities of the design discipline: a critical counterweight to the coming technologies? / Martin Charlier -- Designing human-robot relationships / Scott Stropkay, Bill Hartman -- Tales from the Crick: experiences and services when design meets synthetic biology / Marco Righetto, Andy Goodman -- Beyond 3D printing: the new dimensions of additive fabrication / Steven Keating -- Become an expert at becoming an expert / Lisa deBettencourt -- The changing role of design / Dirk Knemeyer. Subjects: User interfaces (Computer systems)--Design. User interfaces (Computer systems)--Evaluation. User-centered system design. Human-computer interaction. Technological innovations. Human-computer interaction. Technological innovations. User-centered system design. User interfaces (Computer systems)--Design. User interfaces (Computer systems)--Evaluation. Notes: Includes bibliographical references and index.

Devising consumption: cultural economies of insurance, credit and spending LCCN: 2014011352 Personal name: McFall, Elizabeth Rose. Main title: Devising consumption: cultural economies of insurance, credit and spending / Liz Mcfall. Edition: 1 Edition. Published/Produced: New York; London: Routledge, Taylor and Francis Group, 2015 Description: xiii,195 pages; illustrations; 24 cm. Links: Cover image http://images.tandf.co.uk/common/jackets/websmall/978041569/9780415694391.jpg ISBN: 9780415694391 (hardback) LC classification: HG171.M34 2014 Summary: "The book explores the vital role played by the financial service industries in enabling the poor to consume over the last hundred and fifty years. Spending requires means, but these industries offered something else as well - they offered practical marketing devices that captured, captivated and enticed poor consumers. Consumption and consumer markets depend on such devices but their role has been poorly understood both in the social sciences and in business studies and marketing. While the analysis of consumption and markets has been carved up between academics and practitioners who have been interested in either their social and cultural life or their economic and commercial organization, consumption continues to be driven by their combination. Devising consumption requires practical mixtures of commerce and art whether the product is an insurance policy or the next gadget in the internet of things. By making the case for a pragmatic understanding of how ordinary, everyday consumption is orchestrated, the book offers an alternative to orthodox approaches, which should appeal to interdisciplinary audiences interested in questions about how markets work and why it matters"-- Provided by publisher. Subjects: Financial services industry--History. Consumption (Economics) Low-income consumers. Business and Economics / Finance. Political Science / Public Policy / City Planning and Urban Development. History / General. Notes: Includes bibliographical references (pages 176 -190) and index. Series: Culture, Economy and the Social

Digital disciplines: attaining market leadership via the cloud, big data, social, mobile, and the internet of things LCCN: 2015018222 Personal name: Weinman, Joe, 1958- Main title: Digital disciplines: attaining market leadership via the cloud, big data, social, mobile, and the internet of things / Joe Weinman. Published/Produced: Hoboken: Wiley, 2015. Description: pages cm. Links: Cover image http://catalog images.wiley.com/images/db/ji mages/9781118995396.jpg ISBN: 9781118995396 (hardback) LC classification: HF5415.1265 W4525 2015 Summary: "Leverage digital technologies to achieve competitive advantage through better processes, products, customer relationships and innovation How does Information Technology enable competitive advantage? Digital Disciplines details four strategies that exploit today's digital technologies to create unparalleled customer value. Using non-technical language, this book describes the blueprints that any company, large or small, can use to gain or retain market leadership, based on insights derived from examining modern digital giants such as Amazon and Netflix as well as established firms such as GE, Nike, and UPS. Companies can develop a competitive edge through four digital disciplines-- information excellence, solution leadership, collective intimacy, and accelerated innovation--that exploit cloud computing, big data and analytics, mobile and wireline networks, social media, and the Internet of Things. These four disciplines represent the extension and evolution of the value disciplines of operational excellence, product leadership, and customer intimacy originally defined by Michael Treacy and Fred Wiersema in their bestselling business classic The Discipline of Market Leaders. Operational excellence must now encompass information excellence-- leveraging automation, information, analytics, and sophisticated algorithms to make processes faster, better, and more cost-effective, as well as to generate new revenue Product leadership must be extended to solution leadership--smart digital products ranging from wind turbines to wearables connected to each other, cloud services, social networks, and partner ecosystems Customer intimacy is evolving to collective intimacy--as face-to-face relationships not only go online, but are collectively analyzed to provide individually targeted recommendations ranging from books and movies to patient-specific therapies Traditional innovation is no longer enough--accelerated innovation goes beyond open innovation to exploit crowdsourcing, idea markets, challenges, and contest economics to dramatically improve processes, products, and relationships This book provides a strategy framework, empirical data, case studies, deep insights, and pragmatic steps for any enterprise to follow and attain market leadership in today's digital era. Digital Disciplines can be exploited by existing firms or start-ups to disrupt established ways of doing business through innovative, digitally enabled value propositions to win in competitive markets in today's digital era"-- Provided by publisher. Contents: Machine generated contents note: Foreword Preface Acknowledgments Part I: Overview and Background Chapter 1 Digital Disciplines, Strategic Supremacy From Value Disciplines to Digital Disciplines Information Excellence Solution Leadership Collective Intimacy Accelerated Innovation Exponential Value Creation The Leadership Agenda Information Technology in Context Notes Chapter 2 Value Disciplines and Related Frameworks Operational Excellence Product Leadership Customer Intimacy Focus The

Unbundled Corporation
Business Model Generation
Michael Porter and Competitive
Advantage Blue Ocean Strategy
Innovation: The "Fourth" Value
Discipline Notes Chapter 3
Digital Disciplines Information
Excellence Solution Leadership
Collective Intimacy Accelerated
Innovation All of the Above?
Notes Chapter 4 Digital
Technologies The Cloud Big
Data Mobile The Internet of
Things Social Notes Part II:
Information Excellence Chapter
5 Processes, Resources,
Operations and Information
Processes Process Advantage
Process Optimization Asset
Optimization The Business
Value of Information The Role
of Information Technology
Caveats Notes Chapter 6 The
Discipline of Information
Excellence From People to
Machines From Physical to
Virtual From Virtual to Digical
From Processes to Experiences
From Operations to
Improvement From Static
Design to Dynamic
Optimization From Mass
Production to Mass
Personalization From Cost
Reduction to Revenue
Generation From Direct to
Indirect Monetization From
Touchpoints to Integration From
Firms to Networks From Data to

Actionable Insight From
Answers to Exploration Notes
Chapter 7 Burberry--Weaving IT
into the Fabric of the Company
Operational Excellence and
Product Leadership From
Operational Excellence to
Information Excellence From
Physical to Virtual From Virtual
to Digical From Processes to
Experiences From Mass
Production to Mass
Personalization From Cost
Reduction to Revenue
Generation From Touchpoints to
Integration From Firms to
Networks Notes Part III:
Solution Leadership Chapter 8
Products, Services, and
Solutions Competitive Strategy
Product Elements The
Experience Economy Pricing
and Business Models Notes
Chapter 9 The Discipline of
Solution Leadership From
Products and Services to
Solutions From Generic and
Expected to Augmented and
Potential From Transactions to
Relationships From Sales
Results to Customer Outcomes
From Standard Products to
Custom Solutions From
Products and Services to
Experiences and
Transformations From
Standalone to Social From
Product to Platform From
Engineered to Ecosystem Notes

Human Behavior and Gamification Human Behavior Gamification Gamifying Information Excellence Gamifying Solution Leadership Gamifying Collective Intimacy Gamifying Accelerated Innovation Gamification Across Disciplines Notes Chapter 19 Opower--The Power of the Human Mind Human Behavior and Energy Consumption Opower, Information, and Intimacy Notes Chapter 20 Digital Disasters Strategic Errors Cyberattacks Software Design and Development Challenges Operational Issues Unintended Consequences Erratic Algorithms Politics and Pushback Digital Disappointments Notes Part VII: What's Next? Chapter 21 Looking Forward The Exponential Economy Future Technologies Opportunities Critical Success Factors Next Steps Notes About the Author Index. Subjects: Internet marketing. Leadership. Customer services. Business and Economics / Industries / Computer Industry. Notes: Includes index. Additional formats: Online version: Weinman, Joe, 1958- Digital disciplines Hoboken: Wiley, 2015 9781119039884 (DLC)

2015025266 Series: Wiley CIO series

Embedded firmware solutions development best practices for the internet of things LCCN: 2015472110 Personal name: Sun, Jim. Main title: Embedded firmware solutions development best practices for the internet of things / Jiming Sun [and 3 others]. Published/Produced: New York, NY: Apress open, [2015] Description: xxvi, 195 pages; 24 cm ISBN: 9781484200711 (pbk) 1484200713 Subjects: Computer firmware. Internet of things.

Enchanted objects: design, human desire, and the Internet of things LCCN: 2012276721 Personal name: Rose, David, 1967- author. Main title: Enchanted objects: design, human desire, and the Internet of things / David Rose. Edition: First Scribner hardcover edition. Published/Produced: New York, NY: Scribner, [2014]. Description: xiii, 304 pages: illustrations (some color); 24 cm ISBN: 9781476725635 (hardback) 1476725632 (hardback) LC classification: HM851.R665 2014 Summary: We are now standing at the precipice of the next transformative development: the

Internet of Things. Soon, connected technology will be embedded in hundreds of everyday objects we already use: our cars, wallets, watches, umbrellas, even our trash cans. These objects will respond to our needs, come to know us, and learn to think on our behalf. David Rose calls these devices-- which are just beginning to creep into the marketplace-- Enchanted Objects. Some believe the future will look like more of the same--more smartphones, tablets, screens embedded in every conceivable surface. Rose has a different vision: technology that atomizes, combining itself with the objects that make up the very fabric of daily living. Such technology will be woven into the background of our environment, enhancing human relationships and channeling desires for omniscience, long life, and creative expression. The enchanted objects of fairy tales and science fiction will enter real life. Groundbreaking, timely, and provocative, Enchanted Objects is a blueprint for a better future, where efficient solutions come hand in hand with technology that delights our senses. Contents: Prologue: My nightmare -- Part I: Four futures. Terminal world: the domination of glass slabs; Prosthetics: the new bionic you; Animism: living with social robots; Enchanting everyday objects -- Part II: Six human drives. The dialectic interplay: fiction and invention; Drive #1: Omniscience: to know all; Drive #2: Telepathy: human-to-human connections; Drive #3: Safekeeping: protection from all harm; Drive #4: Immortality: a long and quantified life; Drive #5: Teleportation: friction-free travel; Drive #6: Expression: the desire to create -- Part III: The design of enchantment. The extraordinary capability of human senses; Technology sensors and enchanted bricolage; The seven abilities of enchantment. Glanceability; Gestureability; Affordability; Wearability; Indestructibility; Usability; Loveability; Five steps on the ladder of enchantment -- Part IV: Enchanted systems. Transformer homes; Collaborative workplaces; Human-centered cities; Six future fantasies; A metaphor and a macro trend. Subjects: Information technology--Social aspects. Technological innovations-- Social aspects. Internet of things. Embedded Internet devices. Ubiquitous computing. Notes: Includes bibliographical references (pages 277-285) and index.

Exploring BeagleBone: tools and techniques for building with embedded Linux LCCN: 2014951016 Personal name: Molloy, Derek, 1973- author. Main title: Exploring BeagleBone: tools and techniques for building with embedded Linux / Derek Molloy. Published/Produced: Indianapolis, IN: John Wiley and Sons, [2015] Description: xxx, 564 pages: illustrations; 24 cm Links: Cover http://swbplus.bsz-bw.de/bsz426158776cov.htm 20150227150451 ISBN: 9781118935125 (pbk.) 1118935128 (pbk.) LC classification: TK7895.E42 M6556 2015 Contents: The BeagleBone hardware -- The BeagleBone black software -- Exploring embedded Linux systems -- Interfacing electronics -- Practical BeagleBone programming -- Interfacing to the BeagleBone input/outputs -- Cross-compilation and the Eclipse IDE -- Interfacing to the BeagleBone buses -- Interfacing with the physical environment -- The Internet of things -- BeagleBone with a rich user interface -- Images, video, and audio --

Real-time BeagleBone interfacing. Subjects: Linux. Linux. BeagleBone (Computer) Operating systems (Computers) BeagleBone (Computer) Operating systems (Computers) Notes: Includes bibliographical references and index.

From machine-to-machine to the Internet of things: introduction to a new age of intelligence LCCN: 2014469430 Main title: From machine-to-machine to the Internet of things: introduction to a new age of intelligence / Jan Höller [and others]. Published/Produced: Amsterdam: Elsevier Academic Press, 2014. Description: xix, 331 pages: illustrations; 25 cm ISBN: 012407684X (cloth) 9780124076846 (cloth) 0080994016 (electronic bk.) 9780080994017 (electronic bk.) LC classification: TK5105.875.I57 F76 2014 Related names: Höller, Jan. Summary: This book outlines the background and overall vision for the Internet of Things (IoT) and M2M communications and services, including major standards. Key technologies are described: Everything from physical instrumentation devices to the cloud infrastructures used to collect data, derive information and map it to current processes, as well as system architectures and regulatory requirements. Real world service use case studies provide the hands-on knowledge needed to successfully develop and implement M2M and IoT technologies sustainably and profitably. Contents

Hacking h(app)iness: why your personal data counts and how tracking it can change the world LCCN: 2013038876 Personal name: Havens, John C. Main title: Hacking h(app)iness: why your personal data counts and how tracking it can change the world / John C. Havens. Published/Produced: New York: Tarcher, [2014] Description: xxxvi, 268 pages; 24 cm Links: Cover image ftp://ppftpuser: welcome@ftp01.penguingroup.c om/Booksellers and Media/Covers/2008_2009_New _Covers/9780399165313.jpg ISBN: 9780399165313 (hardback) LC classification: HM846.H38 2014 Variant title: Hacking happiness Summary: "In Hacking Happiness, futurist and contributing Mashable writer John C. Havens introduces you to your "quantified self"-your digital identity represented by gigabytes of data produced from tracking your activities on your smartphone and computer. Harvested by megacorporations such as Google, Facebook, and Amazon, Havens argues that companies gather this data because of its immense economic value, encouraging a culture of "sharing" as they hoard the information based on our lives for private monetary gain. But there's an alternative to this digital dystopia. Emerging technologies will help us reclaim this valuable data for ourselves, so we can directly profit from the insights linked to our quantified selves. At the same time, sensors in smartphones and wearable devices will help us track our emotions to improve our well-being based on the science of positive psychology. Havens proposes that these trends will lead to new economic policies that redefine the meaning of "wealth," allowing governments to create policy focused on purpose rather than productivity. An issues book highlighting the benefits of an examined life in the digital world, this timely work takes the trepidation out of the technological renaissance and illustrates how the fruits of the Information Age can improve our lives for a happier humanity"-- Provided by publisher. Contents: Machine generated contents note: Introduction -- SECTION ONE - Identity and Measurement in the Connected World -- Chapter One: Your Identity in the Connected World Chapter Two: Accountability Based Influence Chapter Three: Personal Identity Management Chapter Four: Mobile Sensors Chapter Five: Quantified Self Chapter Six: The Internet of Things Chapter Seven: Artificial Intelligence -- SECTION TWO - Broadcasting Value in the Personal Data Economy -- Chapter Eight: Big Data Chapter Nine: Augmented Reality Chapter Ten: Virtual Currency Chapter Eleven: Shared Value Chapter Twelve: From Consumer to Creator -- SECTION THREE - Promoting Personal and Public Well-Being -- Chapter Thirteen: The Economy of Regard Chapter Fourteen: Positive Psychology Chapter Fifteen: Flow Chapter Sixteen: Altruism Chapter Seventeen: The Value of a Happiness Economy Chapter Eighteen: Beyond GDP Chapter Nineteen: Getting H(app)y Chapter Twenty: Hacking H(app)iness -- SECTION FOUR - Hacking your H(app)iness -- Acknowledgements Endnotes. Subjects: Technological innovations--Social aspects. Self-monitoring. Data mining-- Social aspects. Well-being. Happiness. Technology and Engineering / Social Aspects. Self-Help / Personal Growth / Happiness. Self-Help / Personal Growth / Success.

Handbook of sensor networking: advanced technologies and applications LCCN: 2015451255 Main title: Handbook of sensor networking: advanced technologies and applications / edited by John R. Vacca. Published/Created: Boca Raton, FL: CRC Press, Taylor and Francis Group, [2015] Published/Produced: ©2015 Description: 1 volume (various pagings): illustrations; 26 cm ISBN: 1466569719 9781466569713 LC classification: TK7872.D48 H3578 2015 Related names: Vacca, John R., editor. Contents: Sensor networking internet of things / Lauren Collins -- Sensor network platform and operating systems / Xinheng (Henry) Wang and Shancang Li -- Mobile crowd sensing / Manoop Talasila, Reza Curtmola, and Cristian Borcea -- In-network processing in wireless sensor networks / Qiao Xiang and Hongwei Zhang -- Wireless sensor hierarchical networks / Shancang Li and Xinheng (Henry) Wang -- Efficient distributed Bayesian estimation in wireless sensor networks / Andrew P. Brown, Ronald A. Iltis, and Hua Lee -- Constructing load-balanced data aggregation trees in probabilistic wireless sensor networks / Jing (Selena) He -- Biometric sensors and how they work / Sinjini Mitra -- Radio frequency identification device readers and tags / C.J. Wiemer -- Multimedia/audio sensor networking signal processing / Juan R. Aguilar -- Data mining in sensor networks / Sinjini Mitra and Pramod Pandya -- Wireless sensor network security: PHY-layer security / Andrea Bartoli, Juan Hernandez-Serrano, Miquel Soriano, Mischa Dohler, Apostolos Kountouris, and Dominique Barthel -- Impact of correlated failures on wireless sensor network reliability / Jorge E. Pezoa and Silvia Elena Restrepo -- Acoustic sensors and algorithms for urban security / Juan R. Aguilar -- Smart buildings and smart cities / Rim Boujrad and Thomas M. Chen -- Imaging technology / Hua Lee -- Reconfigurable MIMO FMCW imaging technique and applications in acoustical and microwave imaging / Hua Lee and Michael Lee -- Recent Advances in EO/IR imaging detector and sensor applications / Ashok K. Sood, Yash R. Puri, Nibir K. Dhar, and Dennis L. Polla -- Vehicular sensor networks / Juan Pan and Cristian Borcea -- Acoustic sensing system for underwater geolocation and navigation / Hua Lee -- Load-balanced virtual backbones in wireless sensor networks / Jing (Selena) He -- Appendixes: A. List of sensor networking standards, organizations, and protocols / John R. Vacca -- B. Glossary / John R. Vacca. Subjects: Sensor networks--Handbooks, manuals, etc. Sensor networks. Form/Genre: Handbooks and manuals. Notes: Includes bibliographical references and index.

How mobile devices are changing society LCCN: 2015012262 Personal name: Henderson, Harry. Main title: How mobile devices are changing society / by Harry Henderson. Published/Produced: San Diego, CA: ReferencePoint Press, Inc., 2015. Description: pages cm. ISBN: 9781601529022 (hardback) 1601529023 (hardback) LC classification: HM851.H46 2015 Contents: How did the world become mobile? -- Mobile devices and daily life -- How mobile devices are changing the world -- The future of mobility: wearable devices and the "internet of things". Subjects: Information society--Juvenile literature. Wireless communication systems--Juvenile literature. Notes: Includes bibliographical references and index. Grade 9 to 12. Additional formats: Online version: Henderson, Harry. How mobile devices are changing society San Diego, CA: ReferencePoint Press, Inc., 2015 9781601529039 (DLC) 2015013688 Series: Science, technology, and society

Information security theory and practice: securing the internet of things. 8thIFIP WG 11.2 International Workshop, WISTP 2014, Heraklion, Crete, Greece, June 30 - July 2, 2014. Proceedings LCCN: 2014940797 Main title: Information security theory and practice: securing the internet of things. 8thIFIP WG 11.2 International Workshop, WISTP 2014, Heraklion, Crete, Greece, June 30 - July 2, 2014. Proceedings / [edited by] David Naccache, Damien Sauveron. Edition: 1st edition. Published/Produced: New York: Springer, 2014. Description: pages cm ISBN: 9783662438251 (soft cover: alk.

paper) 3662438259 (soft cover: alk. paper) Series: Lecture notes in computer science; 8501

Internet of things based on smart objects. LCCN: 2014936031 Main title: Internet of things based on smart objects. Published/Produced: New York: Springer, 2014. Description: pages cm Links: Table of contents only http://www.loc.gov/catdir/enhan cements/fy1406/2014936031-t.html Publisher description http://www.loc.gov/catdir/enhan cements/fy1406/2014936031-d.html ISBN: 9783319004907

Internet of things, smart spaces, and next generation networks and systems: 14th International Conference, New2An 2014 and 7th Conference, RUSMART 2014, St. Petersburg, Russia, August 27-28, 2014, Proceedings LCCN: 2014945955 Main title: Internet of things, smart spaces, and next generation networks and systems: 14th International Conference, New2An 2014 and 7th Conference, RUSMART 2014, St. Petersburg, Russia, August 27-28, 2014, Proceedings / [edited by] Sergey Balandin, Sergey Andreev, Yevgeni Koucheryavy. Edition: 1st edition. Published/Produced:

New York: Springer, 2014. Description: pages cm ISBN: 9783319103525 (soft cover: alk. paper) 3319103520 (soft cover: alk. paper) Series: Lecture notes in computer science; 8638

Internet of things, smart spaces, and next generation networks and systems. LCCN: 2015946749 Main title: Internet of things, smart spaces, and next generation networks and systems. Published/Produced: New York, NY: Springer Berlin Heidelberg, 2015. Description: pages cm Links: Publisher description http://www.loc.gov/catdir/enhancements/fy1509/2015946749-d.html ISBN: 9783319231259

Internet of things: challenges and opportunities LCCN: 2014930229 Main title: Internet of things: challenges and opportunities / Subhas Chandra Mukhopadhyay, editor. Published/Produced: Cham: Springer, [2014] Description: viii, 261 pages: illustrations; 25 cm. Links: Table of contents only http://www.loc.gov/catdir/enhancements/fy1412/2014930229-t.html Publisher description http://www.loc.gov/catdir/enhancements/fy1412/2014930229-d.html ISBN: 9783319042220

331904222X LC classification: TK7895.E43 I58 2014 Related names: Mukhopadhyay, Subhas Chandra editor of compilation. Subjects: Embedded Internet devices. Internet of things. Wireless sensor networks. Notes: Includes bibliographical references and index. Series: Smart sensors, measurement and instrumentation; volume 9 Smart sensors, measurement and instrumentation; 9.

Internet of things: emergence, perspectives, privacy and security issues LCCN: 2015472860 Main title: Internet of things: emergence, perspectives, privacy and security issues / Emanuel Delgado, editor. Published/Produced: New York: Nova Science Publishers, [2015] ©2015 Description: viii, 164 pages; 23 cm. ISBN: 1634824423 9781634824422 LC classification: QA76.5915. I58 2015 Related names: Delgado, Emanuel, editor. Contents: Internet of things: privacy and security in a connected world / Federal Trade Commission -- Internet of things workshop report: separate statement of Commissioner Maureen K. Ohlhausen -- Internet of things workshop report: dissenting statement of commissioner Joshua D. Wright -- Careful connections: building security in the Internet of things / Federal Trade Commission -- Testimony of Mike Abbott, General Partner, Kleiner Perkins Caufield and Byers. Hearing on "the Connected World: Examining the Internet of Things" -- Testimony of Justin Brookman, Director, Consumer Privacy, Center for Democracy and Technology. Hearing on "The Connected World: Examining the Internet of Things" -- Statement of Douglas Davis, Vice President and General Manager, Internet of Things Group, Intel. Hearing on "the Connected World: Examining the Internet of Things" -- Testimony of Lance Donny, Chief Executive Officer, OnFarm. Hearing on "The Connected World: Examining the Internet of Things" -- Testimony of Adam Thierer, Senior Research Fellow, Mercatus Center at George Mason University. Hearing on "The Connected World: Examining the Internet of Things." Subjects: Internet of things. Embedded Internet devices. Computer networks--Security measures. Notes: Includes bibliographical references and index. Series: Internet theory, technology and applications Internet theory, technology and applications.

Machine-to-machine communications: architectures, technology, standards, and applications LCCN: 2014008080 Main title: Machine-to-machine communications: architectures, technology, standards, and applications / edited by, Vojislav B. Mišić, Jelena Mišić. Published/Produced: Boca Raton: CRC Press, Taylor and Francis Group, [2015] Description: xvi, 332 pages: illustrations; 24 cm ISBN: 9781466561236 (hardcover: alk. paper) LC classification: TK5105.67.M344 2015 Related names: Mišić, Vojislav B., editor of compilation. Mišić, Jelena, editor of compilation. Subjects: Machine to machine communications. Internet of things. Embedded Internet devices. Telematics. Notes: Includes bibliographical references and index.

Mobile magic: the saatchi and saatchi guide to mobile marketing LCCN: 2013042696 Personal name: Eslinger, Tom. Main title: Mobile magic: the saatchi and saatchi guide to mobile marketing / Tom Eslinger. Edition: First Edition.

Published/Produced: Hoboken: Wiley, [2014]. Description: xv, 234 pages: color illustrations; 23 cm ISBN: 9781118828427 (hardback) LC classification: HF5415.1265.E85 2014 Summary: "A real-world guide to mobile marketing from the head of digital initiatives at Saatchi and Saatchi worldwide The future of marketing is mobile, with seventy-five percent of the world's population having access to a mobile phone and the average American spending 82 minutes per day using her phone for activities other than talking. To traditional marketers unfamiliar with the special challenges of mobile marketing, this territory feels complicated and even frightening. Mobile Magic provides a bird's-eye view of the process of creating great mobile marketing from one of the world's most experienced and successful practitioners"-- Provided by publisher. Contents: Machine generated contents note: Foreword (Kevin Roberts, CEO Worldwide Saatchi and Saatchi) Introduction: Cannes Do 1. Knowing the Terrain Chapter 1: Living in the Screen Age Days of Future's Past The U.S. Plays Catch-up Chapter 2: Why Go Mobile-First? The Mobile Web Why? When? How? Apps vs Mobile Web Your Real-Time Water Cooler Chapter 3: A Crash Course in Mobile Camera Microphone Augmented Reality Accelerometer and Gyroscope Close-range Transmission Processing Power Mobility 2. Understanding the Essentials Chapter 4: The Four Keys to Success Mobile Intimate Social Transactional The Three Ps Checklist Chapter 5: The Sweet Spot Search Just What I Was Looking For All in the Timing Searching for the Answers Social Joining, Having and Starting Conversations More Isn't Always Merrier Look, Listen, Participate The Sweet Spot Dashboard Tools for Monitoring and Distribution: the Non-Mobile Part of Mobile. Chapter 6: Know Thyself (And Thy Audience) Know Your Persona Know Your Voice Know Your Ecosystem Know Your Audience Know Why You're There Chapter 7: Location, Location, Very Specific Location Do I Need a Location-based Component to My App? Surprise and Delight A Short Radius Goes a Long Way Cumulative Location-Tracking The Creep Factor: When Location Goes Too Far Getting Permission 3. Getting Going Chapter 8: How to

Budget The Two Components of a Mobile Budget How Much Money Should I Plan to Spend on Mobile? Taking Inventory of Your Mobile Infrastructure Determining Your Budget: Rule of Thumb Complexity Equals Cost Budgeting for Staff Mobile Commerce and Budgeting for Immediate Returns Do Your Research Investing in involvement Hidden Costs The Complexity Scale Budget for Success The Power of Love / Love Don't Cost a Thing Chapter 9: Build Your Team The Research The Interviews The Selection Warning Signs So What Role Do I Play in This? Chapter 10: Interfacing With Design The Success Metric Start with What You Know: The Style Guide Getting the Ball Rolling: The Brief Fingers, Not Eyes: User Flow Diagrams and Wire Frames Do What You Gotta Do Chapter 11: Making the Stuff Know Your Scale Production Part 1: Optimize that Website! Part 2: The Appropriate Next Step What Makes a Good App? Don't Forget About Desktop! Text-Based Marketing An Ethical Law-Abiding Mobile Effort 4. Being and Staying Attractive Chapter 12: Lovemarks Mystery: What's the Story? Sensuality Intimacy Mobile Lovemarks: Lovemark- ception Chapter 13: Communication With Your Audience Keep it on the Straight and Narrow Don't Trick People! Don't Be Coy. Be Relevant. Own Up to Your Mistakes. Time to Shut it Down: Planned Obsolescence The Obsolescence Sine Curve Tell It Straight, Tell It Plain Chapter 14: Selling Everything Everywhere The Perpetual Path to Purchase Showrooming: Where Mobile and Real-World Butt Heads The Long and Winding Road Bring the Store to Them Mobile Magic 5. Ensuring Success Chapter 15: The Finish Line Legal Not Supporting Your Campaign How to Keep Interest in your Mobile App Trying to Do Too Much Chapter 16: Measuring Success Investment vs Involvement Defining the Success Metric Mobile Success as Part of the Larger Picture Finger on the Pulse Lovemarks Return on Involvement Chapter 17.1: Case Story Case Story: Chase for the Charms from Saatchi and Saatchi and Lucky Charms Chapter 17.2: Case Story Case Story: The Tori 500 from Team One and Lexus Chapter 17.3: Case Story Tag the Weather from Saatchi and Saatchi Stockholm and P and G Nordic Chapter 18: The Future The Language of Mobile The

Internet of Things Augmented Everything Autonomous Autos Gaming the Gamer Data-Driven Everything Divergence Theory: The Wild World of Mobile Making Mobile Magic. Subjects: Telemarketing. Internet marketing. Branding (Marketing) Business and Economics / Advertising and Promotion. Notes: Includes index. Additional formats: Online version: Eslinger, Tom. Mobile magic First Edition. Hoboken: Wiley, 2014 9781118855188 (DLC) 2014000199

NGN architectures, protocols, and services LCCN: 2014005793 Personal name: Janevski, Toni. Main title: NGN architectures, protocols, and services / Toni Janevski. Published/Produced: Chichester, West Sussex, United Kingdom: Wiley, 2014. Description: xiii, 352 pages: illustrations; 26 cm Links: Cover image http://catalogimages.wiley.com/images/db/jimages/9781118607206.jpg ISBN: 9781118607206 (hardback) LC classification: TK5105.5.J358 2014 Summary: "Comprehensive coverage explaining the correlation and synergy between Next Generation Networks and the existing standardized technologies. This book focuses on Next Generation Networks (NGN); in particular, on NGN architectures, protocols and services, including technologies, regulation and business aspects. NGN provides convergence between the traditional telecommunications and the Internet, and it is globally standardized by the ITU (International Telecommunication Union), where ITU is the United Nations specialized agency for Information and Communication Technologies - ICTs. The convergence towards the NGN is based on the Internet technologies, and the introductory chapters cover the Internet fundamentals of today, including architectures, protocols (IPv4, IPv6, TCP, DNS, etc.), Internet services (WWW, e-mail, BitTorrent, Skype, and more), as well as Internet governance. Further, the prerequisite for convergence of all ICT services over single network architectures is broadband access to the Internet. Hence, the book includes architectures of fixed broadband Internet access networks, such as DSL (Digital Subscriber Line) networks, cable networks, FTTH (Fiber To The Home), next generation passive and active optical networks, and metro Ethernet. It also covers network architectures for next generation (4G) mobile and wireless networks (LTE/LTE-Advanced, and Mobile WiMAX 2.0), then Fixed Mobile Convergence - FMC, next generation mobile services, as well as business and regulatory aspects for next generation mobile networks and services. Comprehensive coverage explaining the correlation and synergy between Next Generation Networks and the existing standardized technologies Focuses on Next Generation Networks (NGN) as defined by the ITU, including performance, service architectures and mechanisms, common IMS (IP Multimedia Subsystem), control and signalling protocols used in NGN, security approaches, identity management, NGN Service Overlay Networks, and NGN business models Examines the most important NGN services, including QoS-enabled VoIP, IPTV over NGN, web services in NGN, peer-to-peer services, Ubiquitous Sensor Network (USN) services, VPN services in NGN, Internet of things and web of things Includes the transition towards NGN from the PSTN (Public Switched Telephone Networks)

and from the best-effort Internet via the same Internet access Explores advanced topics such as IPv6-based NGN, network virtualization, and future packet based networks, as well as business challenges and opportunities for the NGN evolved networks and services Essential reading for engineers and employees from regulatory bodies, government organisations, telecommunication companies, ICT companies"-- Provided by publisher. Subjects: Computer networks--Technological innovations--Forecasting. Technology and Engineering / Telecommunications. Notes: Includes bibliographical references and index. Additional formats: Online version: Janevski, Toni. NGN architectures, protocols, and services Chichester, West Sussex, United Kingdom: John Wiley and Sons Inc., 2014 9781118607367 (DLC) 2014014870

Pax technica: how the internet of things may set us free or lock us up LCCN: 2014040794 Personal name: Howard, Philip N. Main title: Pax technica: how the internet of things may set us free or lock us up / Philip N. Howard. Published/Produced:

New Haven: London: Yale University Press, [2015] Description: xxv, 320 pages; 22 cm ISBN: 9780300199475 (hardback) LC classification: HM851.H69 2015 Summary: "Should we fear or welcome the internet's evolution? The "internet of things" is the rapidly growing network of everyday objects--eyeglasses, cars, thermostats--made smart with sensors and internet addresses. Soon we will live in a pervasive yet invisible network of everyday objects that communicate with one another. In this original and provocative book, Philip N. Howard envisions a new world order emerging from this great transformation in the technologies around us. Howard calls this new era a Pax Technica. He looks to a future of global stability built upon device networks with immense potential for empowering citizens, making government transparent, and broadening information access. Howard cautions, however, that privacy threats are enormous, as is the potential for social control and political manipulation. Drawing on evidence from around the world, he illustrates how the internet of things can be used to repress and control people. Yet he also demonstrates that if we actively engage with the governments and businesses building the internet of things, we have a chance to build a new kind of internet--and a more open society"-- Provided by publisher. Subjects: Internet--Social aspects. Information technology--Political aspects. Technological innovations--Political aspects. Privacy, Right of. Electronic surveillance. Social Science / Media Studies. Technology and Engineering / Telecommunications. Notes: Includes bibliographical references and index.

Principles of cyber-physical systems LCCN: 2014039755 Personal name: Alur, Rajeev, 1966- Main title: Principles of cyber-physical systems / Rajeev Alur. Published/Produced: Cambridge, Massachusetts: The MIT Press, [2015] Description: xii, 446 pages: illustrations; 24 cm ISBN: 9780262029117 (hardcover: alk. paper) LC classification: TJ213.A365 2015 Subjects: Automatic control. System design. Embedded internet devices. Internet of things. Formal methods (Computer science) Notes: Includes bibliographical references and index.

Resource revolution: how to capture the biggest business opportunity in a century LCCN: 2013362496 Personal name: Heck, Stefan, 1970- author. Main title: Resource revolution: how to capture the biggest business opportunity in a century / Stefan Heck and Matt Rogers with Paul Carroll. Published/Produced: Boston: Houghton Mifflin Harcourt, 2014. Description: xii, 256 pages: illustrations; 24 cm Links: Publisher description http://www.loc.gov/catdir/enhancements/fy1408/2013362496-d.html Contributor biographical information http://www.loc.gov/catdir/enhancements/fy1408/2013362496-b.html ISBN: 9780544114562 0544114566 LC classification: HF1008.H43 2014 Related names: Rogers, Matt, author. Carroll, Paul, author. Contents: Capturing the greatest business opportunity in a century -- Joysticks meet drilling rigs, launching the revolution -- The recipe for tenfold resource productivity improvement -- DIRTT and software: assembly required -- System integration: the power of machines meets the internet of things -- Timing is everything -- Making it matter: scaling and commercialization -- Organizing for success -- Go big or go home. Subjects: Business enterprises. Commerce. Natural resources--Management. Commercial products. Notes: Includes bibliographical references and index.

Smart cities: big data, civic hackers, and the quest for a new utopia LCCN: 2015295920 Personal name: Townsend, Anthony M., 1973- Main title: Smart cities: big data, civic hackers, and the quest for a new utopia / Anthony M. Townsend. Published/Produced: New York: W.W. Norton and Company, [2014] Description: xiv, 388 pages; 25 cm ISBN: 9780393349788 0393349780 LC classification: HT119.T65 2014 Summary: We live in a world defined by urbanization and digital ubiquity, where mobile broadband connections outnumber fixed ones, machines dominate a new "Internet of things," and more people live in cities than in the countryside. In Smart Cities, urbanist and technology expert Anthony Townsend takes a broad historical look at the forces that have shaped the planning and design of cities and information technologies from the rise of the great industrial cities of the nineteenth century to the present. A century ago, the telegraph and the mechanical tabulator were used to tame cities of millions. Today, cellular networks and cloud computing tie together the complex choreography of mega-regions of tens of millions of people. In response, cities worldwide are deploying technology to address both the timeless challenges of government and the mounting problems posed by human settlements of previously unimaginable size and complexity. In Chicago, GPS sensors on snow plows feed a real-time "plow tracker" map that everyone can access. In Zaragoza, Spain, a "citizen card" can get you on the free city-wide Wi-Fi network, unlock a bike share, check a book out of the library, and pay for your bus ride home. In New York, a guerrilla group of citizen-scientists installed sensors in local sewers to alert you when stormwater runoff overwhelms the system, dumping waste into local waterways. As technology barons, entrepreneurs, mayors, and an emerging vanguard of civic hackers are trying to shape this new frontier, Smart Cities considers the motivations, aspirations, and shortcomings of them all while offering a new civics to guide our efforts as we build the future together, one click at a time. -- Provided by publisher. Contents: Urbanization and ubiquity -- The $100 billion jackpot -- Cybernetics redux -- Cities of tomorrow -- The open-source metropolis -- Tinkering toward utopia -- Have nots -- Reinventing city hall -- A planet of civic laboratories -- Buggy, brittle, and bugged -- A new civics for a smart century. Subjects: Cities and towns-- History. City planning-- Technological innovations. Regional planning-- Technological innovations. Technological innovations-- Economic aspects. Information technology--Economic aspects. Technologies de l'information et de la communication. Innovations technologiques. Villes. Aménagement urbain. Planification régionale. Société de l'information. Aspects économiques. Cities and towns. City planning--Technological innovations. Information technology--Economic aspects. Regional planning-- Technological innovations. Technological innovations-- Economic aspects. Digitaltechnik. Informationstechnik. Stadtplanung. Form/Genre: History. Notes: "With a new epilogue"--Cover. "First published as a Norton paperback 2014"--Title page verso. Includes bibliographical references (pages 329-370) and index.

Smart machines and the Internet of things LCCN: 2015021316 Personal name: Nagelhout, Ryan. Main title: Smart machines and the Internet of things / Ryan Nagelhout. Edition: First Edition. Published/Produced: New York: Rosen Publishing, 2015. Description: pages cm. ISBN: 9781499437799 (library bound) 9781499437775 (pbk.) 9781499437782 (6-pack) LC classification: QA76.5915.N34 2015 Contents: ARPANET to Internet -- Screens to things -- The smart home -- The smart world -- The future of things. Subjects: Internet of things-- Juvenile literature. Notes: Includes bibliographical references and index. Series: Digital and information literacy

Smart SysTech 2015: European Conference on Smart Objects, Systems, and Technologies, June 16-17, 2015 in Aachen, Germany LCCN: 2015417167 Meeting name: Smart SysTech (Conference) (2015: Aachen, Germany) Main title: Smart SysTech 2015: European Conference on Smart Objects, Systems, and Technologies, June 16-17, 2015 in Aachen, Germany / organized in cooperation with RWTH Aachen University, Aachen, Germany, Association for Automatic Identification and Mobile Data Capture (AIM), Information Technology Society within VDE (ITG). Published/Produced: Berlin: VDE-Verlag, [2015] ©2015 Description: 1 CD-ROM: color; 4 3/4 in. ISBN: 9783800739967 LC classification: TK6570.I34 Related names: Rheinisch-Westfälische Technische Hochschule Aachen, organizer. AIM-Deutschland e.V., organizer. Informationstechnische Gesellschaft im VDE, organizer. Subjects: Radio frequency identification systems-- Congresses. Detectors-- Congresses. Internet of things-- Congresses. Notes: Title from disc label. Includes bibliographical references. Series: ITG-Fachbericht, 0932-6022; 259

The internet of things LCCN: 2014042259 Personal name: Greengard, Samuel. Main title: The internet of things / Samuel Greengard. Published/Produced: Cambridge, Massachusetts: MIT

Press, [2015] Description: xviii, 210 pages; 18 cm. ISBN: 9780262527736 (pbk.: alk. paper) LC classification: TK7895.E43 G74 2015 Contents: The internet changes everything -- Mobility, clouds, and digital tools usher in a connected world -- The industrial internet emerges -- Computer devices get smart -- Putting the internet of things to work -- The reality and repercussions of a connected world -- A networked future emerges. Subjects: Embedded computer systems--Popular works. Internet of things--Popular works. Notes: Includes bibliographical references (pages 201-202) and index. Series: MIT press essential knowledge series

The Internet of things: do-it-yourself projects with Arduino, Raspberry Pi, and Beaglebone Black LCCN: 2015451621 Personal name: Norris, Donald (Electrical engineer), author. Main title: The Internet of things: do-it-yourself projects with Arduino, Raspberry Pi, and Beaglebone Black / Donald Norris. Published/Produced: New York: McGraw-Hill Education, 2015. ©2015 Description: xv, 336 pages: illustrations; 23 cm Links: Contributor biographical information http://www.loc.gov/catdir/enhancements/fy1510/2015451621-b.html Publisher description http://www.loc.gov/catdir/enhancements/fy1510/2015451621-d.html Table of contents only http://www.loc.gov/catdir/enhancements/fy1510/2015451621-t.html ISBN: 9780071835206 0071835202 LC classification: QA76.8.R19 N66 2015 Summary: The Internet of Things gets you started working with the most popular processing platforms and wireless communication technologies to connect devices and systems to the Internet using sensors. You'll learn the basics of object-oriented programming and relational databases so you can complete your projects with ease. Each project features a list of required tools and components, how-to explanations with photos and illustrations, and complete programming code. Take advantage of the power and versatility of the IoT with help from this practical, easy-to-follow guide. Subjects: Programmable controllers--Programming. Arduino (Programmable controller)--Programming. Raspberry Pi (Computer)--Programming.

BeagleBone Black (Computer)--
Programming. Notes: Includes
index. Subtitle of electronic
version reads; "do-it-yourself at
home projects for Arduino,
Raspberry Pi, and Beaglebone"

The Internet of things: how smart
TVs, smart cars, smart homes,
and smart cities are changing the
world LCCN: 2015932632
Personal name: Miller, Michael,
1958- author. Main title: The
Internet of things: how smart
TVs, smart cars, smart homes,
and smart cities are changing the
world / Michael Miller.
Published/Produced:
Indianapolis, Indiana: Que,
[2015] Description: xiii, 319
pages: illustrations; 23 cm
ISBN: 9780789754004
0789754002 LC classification:
TK7895.E43 M55 2015
Subjects: Embedded Internet
devices. Machine-to-machine
communications. Internet of
things. Ubiquitous computing.
Internet of things. Ubiquitous
computing. Notes: Includes
index.

The power of mobile banking: how
to profit from the revolution in
retail financial series LCCN:
2014012629 Personal name:
Krishnan, Sankar, 1967- Main
title: The power of mobile
banking: how to profit from the

revolution in retail financial
series / Sankar Krishnan.
Published/Produced: Hoboken,
New Jersey: Wiley, [2014]
Description: xix, 172 pages; 24
cm ISBN: 9781118914243
(hardback) LC classification:
HG1708.7.K75 2014 Summary:
"Two disruptions of absolutely
unimaginable scale are radically
and totally transforming retail
banking: (1) a worldwide
convergence of financial
services, telecom, retail,
healthcare and media and (2) the
chaotic mash-up of multiple
emerging phenomena including
nanotechnology, big data
analytics, telemedicine, smart
cities, machine-to-machine
interaction (the Internet of
Things) and the incredibly rapid
growth of the middleclass in
Asia, South Asia and parts of
Africa. The new middleclass
represents hundreds of billions
of dollars in fresh revenue for
retail banks. By training and
temperament, however, most
retail bankers are unable to
"think beyond the branch." They
do not understand that in the
modern connected world, the
"branch" is becoming largely
irrelevant. What matters instead
are the services delivered to your
laptop, your tablet and your
smart phone. Connected digital
devices are the future of retail

banking, and the time to begin preparing for the new paradigm in right now! The book provides the steps necessary for a retail bank to adapt, evolve, and succeed in the new world"-- Provided by publisher. "Provides a detailed roadmap for survival and success in the increasingly perilous and risky world of retail banking"-- Provided by publisher. Subjects: Internet banking. Banks and banking. Business and Economics / Banks and Banking. Notes: Includes bibliographical references and index. Additional formats: Online version: Krishnan, Sankar, 1967- Profitable banking Hoboken: Wiley, 2014 9781118932032 (DLC) 2014017629

The shaping of ambient intelligence and the internet of things. LCCN: 2015953003 Main title: The shaping of ambient intelligence and the internet of things. Published/Produced: New York, NY: Springer Berlin Heidelberg, 2015. Description: pages cm ISBN: 9789462391413

The vision for moving from M2M to IoT -- Introduction and book structure -- M2M to IoT -- the vision -- M2M to IoT -- A market perspective -- M2M to IoT -- an architectural overview -- 2. IOT Technologies and architectures -- M2M and IoT technology fundamentals -- IoT architecture -- state of the art -- Architecture reference model -- IoT reference architecture -- Real-world design constraints -- 3. IOT use cases -- Asset management -- Industrial automation -- The smart grid -- Commercial building automation -- Smart cities -- Participatory sensing -- Conclusion and looking ahead. Subjects: Machine-to-machine communications. Internet of things. Notes: Includes bibliographical references and index.

The zero marginal cost society: the internet of things, the collaborative commons, and the eclipse of capitalism LCCN: 2013033940 Personal name: Rifkin, Jeremy. Main title: The zero marginal cost society: the internet of things, the collaborative commons, and the eclipse of capitalism / Jeremy Rifkin. Published/Produced: New York: Palgrave Macmillan, 2014. Description: 356 pages; 25 cm ISBN: 9781137278463 (hardcover: alk. paper) LC classification: HB501.R555 2014 Subjects: Capitalism. Cost.

Cooperation. Notes: Includes bibliographical references (pages 343-347) and index.

Understanding context: environment, language, and information architecture LCCN: 2015430390 Personal name: Hinton, Andrew (Information architect), author. Main title: Understanding context: environment, language, and information architecture / Andrew Hinton. Edition: First edition. Published/Produced: Sebastopol, CA: O'Reilly Media, Inc., 2014. ©2015. Description: xx, 440 pages: illustrations (some color); 23 cm Links: Cover http://swbplus.bsz-bw.de/bsz408477636cov.htm 20140630161225 ISBN: 9781449323172 1449323170 LC classification: QA76.9.H85 H565 2014 Summary: "This practical, insightful book provides a powerful toolset to help information architects, UX professionals, and web and app designers understand and solve the many challenges of contextual ambiguity in the products and services they create. You'll discover not only how to design for a given context, but also how design participates in making context. Learn how people perceive context when touching and navigating digital environments.

See how labels, relationships, and rules work as building blocks for context. Find out how to make better sense of cross-channel, multi-device products or services. Discover how language creates infrastructure in organizations, software, and the Internet of Things. Learn models for figuring out the contextual angles of any user experience"--Back cover. Subjects: Interpersonal communication. Communication--Study and teaching. Information storage and retrieval systems--Architecture. Web sites--Design. Communication--Study and teaching. Information storage and retrieval systems--Architecture. Interpersonal communication. Web sites--Design. Notes: Includes bibliographical references and index.

Value creation and the Internet of things: how the behavior economy will shape the 4th industrial revolution LCCN: 2015003792 Personal name: Manu, Alexander, 1954- Main title: Value creation and the Internet of things: how the behavior economy will shape the 4th industrial revolution / Alexander Manu. Published/Produced: Farnham,

Surrey, England; Burlington,
VT: Gower, [2015] Description:
viii, 233 pages; 25 cm ISBN:
9781472451811 (hardback: alk.
paper) LC classification:
HC79.T4 M3487 2015 Subjects:
Technological innovations--
Economic aspects. New
products. Value. Consumption
(Economics)--Psychological
aspects. Notes: Includes
bibliographical references
(pages 209- 216) and index.

INDEX

D

E